The Barnabas Way

© 2018 by Isaac Smythia

ISmythia1@gmail.com

In many of the personal examples and illustrations, names and identifying information have been changed to protect the individuals' privacy.

ISBN: 978-1-5323-6212-3

Printed in the U.S.A.

THE BARNABAS WAY

A NEW PERSPECTIVE ON BIBLICAL LEADERSHIP

ISAAC SMYTHIA

Endorsements

I enjoy reading books where the author's words are more than theory; they are values that are being lived out. The Barnabas Way is authored by a true modern day Barnabas. I have witnessed Isaac Smythia as a leader, pastor, missionary, and ministry field representative. In each of these roles, I've observed the principles he writes about in action in his ministry. The Barnabas Way is a call to see things that no one else sees, and to do things that no one else does.

Doug Clay (General Superintendent of the Assemblies of God)

Every Christ-follower will be profoundly encouraged by the powerful insights that only someone of Isaac Smythia's heart and experience can deliver. It's as though the author conveys the very nature of Barnabas's character in a way that will have readers realizing that they themselves have somehow stepped into Paul's role as a young apprentice. If you know a young minister, missionary or even a young Christian, do them and the body of Christ a favor by getting a copy of this treasure into their hands!

John Wootton (Superintendent, Ohio Ministry Network of the Assemblies of God)

Isaac Smythia writes with the authority of one who has not only studied the story of Barnabas, but has lived out The Barnabas Way in ministry. Isaac begins each chapter as a story teller, describing the "in between the lines" of the biblical text, getting into the mind and heart of Barnabas. The remainder of each chapter is rich in spiritual leadership truths that are valuable to us all. You will appreciate the truths of each chapter in The Barnabas Way regardless of your ministry, position or years as a follower of Jesus.

Dave Ellis (Regional Director for Latin American and the Caribbean for Assemblies of God World Missions)

I have worked with Missionary/Leader Isaac Smythia for nearly 30 years. He is a dedicated practitioner of missions and ministry. I agreed to review The Barnabas Way thinking I would quickly scan through it. However, from the very opening portions of this work I was transported into the story of Barnabas. The applications Isaac pulls from Barnabas' story are replete with every day helps for leaders of every level. I recommend this book to you and am sure you will enjoy it and profit from it as I have already!

Jeffrey Dove (Missions Leader, Director of Life Publishers International and the Assemblies of God Bible Alliance)

"Coaching" is not a new phenomenon. It is an age old biblical principle modeled throughout the pages of scripture. In The Barnabas Way, Isaac Smythia captures the heart of one of the all-time great coaches, Barnabas. The book's simple concepts can be used by any coach to bring out the God-given potential in those they lead. More than just theory, they are proven principles that Smythia used to help ten young, inexperienced Uruguayan pastors become successful church planters. The Barnabas Way will help anyone interested in leading others on their journey toward greatness.

Randy Carter (Lead Pastor, Northside Assembly, Jackson, Tennessee)

I plan to use The Barnabas Way as a teaching resource with my Church Staff and Ministry Teams. Barnabas has much to offer when it comes to leadership lessons and Isaac Smythia draws out the best of those lessons. The book is not just full of good ideas and theories, but also practical leadership principles that can help bring life transformation for the sake of the Kingdom. Sharing from his vast experiences in a variety of leadership settings Isaac outlines his ministry leadership philosophy rooted in the life of Barnabas.

Gordon McClure (Senior Pastor, Emanuel Church, Abilene, Kansas)

Foreword

We pulled up to the small house on a dirt road in a place I had never been before. I found myself apprehensive of what might happen next. The 12 hour flight from the United States to Uruguay had left me tired and off balance. As I climbed out of the missionary's vehicle, I watched as he walked up to the home we were visiting. A big smile on his face, he clapped his hands, calling out words of affirmation before we ever reached the door. The young couple's eyes lit up when they opened the door, saw him standing there, and invited us in.

For the most part, the language barrier left me an outsider to their conversation. But from the tone of their voices and the looks on their faces, it wasn't hard for me to understand what they were talking about. There were moments of serious dialog about the young couple's responsibilities leading the new church plant and the life these newlyweds were starting together. Laughter led to teary eyes as the missionary spoke a language that needed no interpretation. He was imparting life into this couple, giving them a great gift that they would cling on to through the challenging times ahead of them. It was the language of encouragement.

Fast forward months later to a restaurant in Ohio. That same missionary sat with a young pastor who was facing some of the most challenging decisions of his new position. No matter what choices would be made, painful consequences lay ahead for the people involved. Although he may not have realized it that morning, that pastor needed someone to speak life and wisdom to him.

The missionary leaned across the table, looked that young pastor in the eyes and began to impart words of life straight from the Holy Spirit. It didn't make the decisions any easier, but it did give that pastor the courage to move forward with what was best for the church. Isaac Smythia was that missionary who spoke the language of encouragement to me that morning.

I have been privileged to travel with Isaac on three continents. No matter where he goes, he speaks this language that people understand. Isaac has learned what it means to lead others to a place where they can see God's love for them and believe that God has great things in store for them. Whether it is the child who needs a laugh, or the young church planter who is questioning their calling, or the tired individual who needs someone to believe in them, Isaac speaks loud and clear the language of encouragement.

The Barnabas Way does not just a retell a Bible story. This book is the result of a life-long study of life-giving leadership principles. If you looked at Isaac's resume, it would speak of his time as local church pastor, Bible school leader, church planter and substance abuse recovery center director. His education would tell you he is a trained pastor, counselor and missionary. But what makes Isaac a great example and leader in the Kingdom of God is the language he speaks better than anyone else I know, the language of encouragement.

The New Testament's story of Barnabas tells us about the encourager who shaped the course of church history. His willingness to invest in the life of others had an impact that we will only fully appreciate when we get to Heaven. My prayer is that you also will become fluent in the language of encouragement as you spend time learning The Barnabas Way.

Chad Gilligan (Lead Pastor, Calvary Church, Maumee, Ohio)

For Terry

The light of my life after Jesus Christ

Acknowledgments

For me writing a book is like preparing fine meal with many courses. The process of buying, preparing, and cooking is often forgotten as soon as the last plate and spoon are washed and put away. Only the cook remembers each step and truly appreciates those who helped make the feast a reality.

Thank you to the small knot of people who helped make this book a reality. Doug Clay made me sign a promissory note that I would finish writing the long delayed last chapters. Beth Veller did the first corrections on the manuscript. Angela Kingsriter formatted the book and designed the cover. My editor, Tracey Moore, spent countless hours editing and helping me rewrite many portions and refine The Barnabas Way. *I so appreciate each of you!*

Finally, I thank our heavenly Father. He drew my attention to Barnabas' story many years ago, showed me what an amazing leader this apostle was, and inspired me to write The Barnabas Way.

Table of Contents

Introduction

When he (Saul) had come to Jerusalem... Barnabas took him

The Middle Eastern man pulled his prayer shawl over his head and peeked around the corner again. He watched the young Pharisee absentmindedly kicking at the dust with his sandal before sitting beside the community well, looking around. The Pharisee's dark eyes squinted as they roamed back and forth over the square, searching, waiting. The young man was well dressed, a little on the short side, with just the beginnings of a bald spot.

He appeared to be alone, but how could one be sure? It could be a trap. The young man's reputation was certainly well known. The watcher hesitated, pulling his shawl a little tighter around his head. A bead of sweat trickled down his neck in the afternoon sun as he watched. So much was at stake, and the leaders did not trust this supposed new follower of Messiah. Yet there was something about this young man. It was more than a hunch but not quite enough to keep nagging doubts from plaguing the watcher's mind.

"Father," he prayed, "You know all things. I ask that You guide me, protect me, and give me wisdom." He took a deep breath, then slowly pulled the shawl from his face as he stepped around the corner and toward the well. His voice sounded more confident than he really felt as he called out, "Brother Saul, my name is Barnabas."

(Based on Acts 9:26–27)

Which came first—the apple or the tree? The chicken or the egg? There is no question for those who acknowledge God as creator. God created trees, chickens, plants, animals, and humans, all with a mandate to reproduce through their seed. If you trace the seeds of the church to its beginnings, you will find Jesus

Christ, the author and the finisher of our faith. He did more than just give His life on the cross. He invested three years of His time on earth into the lives of His disciples, who then took the good news of His kingdom from Jerusalem to Judea, to Samaria, and to the uttermost parts of the earth.

After Christ, who was the most influential leader of the early church? Many would point to the apostle Paul. Paul spread the gospel first to Turkey and then into Europe. He testified to kings and rulers of the power of Jesus Christ, and his letters make up a major portion of the New Testament.

But if you take a step back in your thinking, another early church leader may come to mind. Barnabas saw something in Saul when the apostles were unwilling to meet with the young man. Later, when Saul had been sent home after stirring up problems for the struggling new church in Jerusalem, Barnabas went to Tarsus to look for him. Barnabas also took Saul with him on the first missionary journey.

John Mark was another young Christian leader whose life was greatly influenced by Barnabas. Most recognize Mark's book as the first Gospel to be written; 93 percent of it was used in the writings of Matthew and Luke. John Mark is also known for founding the powerful church in Alexandria, Egypt, opening the door for the spread of the gospel into Africa.

This is the same Mark who abandoned Barnabas and Paul during their first missionary journey. Later, Barnabas insisted on giving Mark a second chance despite Paul's vehement opposition. Paul could not see beyond Mark's desertion on the shores of modern-day Turkey. Yet Barnabas saw something Paul couldn't see, and he paid a heavy price for his vision. After a heated argument between the two apostles, Paul and Barnabas separated. Paul took Silas for the journeys described in the remainder of Acts. Barnabas took Mark with him to Cyprus and disappeared from the pages of Scripture.

Only God truly knows what might have happened in Paul's life without Barnabas' influence. We can only speculate whether Mark would have written his Gospel or traveled to Africa had it not been for Barnabas' intervention in his life. Yet we do know Barnabas shaped the lives of these two Christian leaders. His leadership sowed seeds that bore much fruit, as together Paul and Mark wrote almost a third of the New Testament and planted churches from Europe to Africa.

So which came first or had more impact? The apple or the tree? These two key leaders of the New Testament church or their mentor? Whatever your answer, I believe Barnabas gives us a unique perspective of biblical leadership. There are many ways to consider and learn about leadership in the church—books, sermons, Power Point presentations, and so on. This is simply what I call the Barnabas Way.

The seed for this book was first planted in my life years ago when I began to consider what the statement in Acts 11:25, "Then Barnabas went to Tarsus to look for Saul," meant not only for Paul but also for Barnabas. Three powerful facts sprouted from the Word. First, *Barnabas saw what no one else saw*, first in Saul and then in Mark. Second, *Barnabas did what no one else would do*. When the original apostles and later Paul refused to do so, Barnabas mentored two young Christ followers who had experienced significant setbacks in their ministries. Finally, *Barnabas paid a price that others wouldn't pay*. He left Jerusalem to an unknown future in Antioch. He then gave up his leadership position in Antioch to take Paul on their historic first missionary journey. Later, he left his position with Paul to start the process all over again with Mark.

The Barnabas Way follows the life of Barnabas in the book of Acts, gleaning the biblical leadership principles he leaves in his wake. The fictional vignettes at the beginning of each chapter illustrate what Barnabas may have experienced during his ministry. They are nothing more than my attempt to color in some detail to the broad strokes of the biblical record.

In this book I look at Barnabas' leadership through the lens of my own experiences. Many of the illustrations come from my wife's and my twenty-five years of missionary work in Uruguay and other parts of the world. My prayer is that you will take a new look at Barnabas' story through your own lens and draw lessons that will help you influence those who are building the Kingdom with you.

Start

*Barnabas... sold a field that belonged to him
and brought the money and laid it at the apostles' feet*

*As he stood near the back of the group, Joseph's head swam
as he tried to organize the whirl of memories from the past
weeks in his mind. He could still see the flames on everyone's
heads when the Spirit had first come upon them. Someone
had told him he had one over his head too, but he hadn't felt
anything. Actually, he had felt everything—the joy, the wonder, the pressure deep inside that had birthed the strange
language pouring from his mouth. Barely able to stand, he
had opened his eyes a few times to see others staggering as
well. He didn't know how long it had lasted, only that when
Peter had begun to address the gawking crowd, the sense of
floating in God's presence had started to abate and Joseph
could feel his feet on the ground once again.*

*It was almost the same every time the believers gathered,
sometimes in houses, other times in the temple. It didn't
matter—everyone knew that when they came together
something was going to happen. The 120 in the upper room
became thousands. Beggars and prostitutes, Pharisees and
priests were baptized and then stood side by side in awe and
worship. Old psalms sung in tired rituals suddenly became
the Spirit's chariots of praise that lifted the singers into
the presence of God. The stories and words of the prophets
burned with new fire.*

*It was amazing. It was also terrible. The Sanhedrin was
stiffening its resistance. No one could deny the miraculous
healing of the beggar outside the temple, yet Peter and John
were arrested and threatened. Other followers of Messiah*

were thrown out of their synagogues. There were rumors of a special group of Pharisees going from synagogue to synagogue to get rid of the people of the Way. Families fractured as parents, spouses, and even children turned against loved ones who dared to confess Jesus as Lord. Believers' homes opened to receive those who had nowhere else to go. But so many more now-dispossessed followers of Christ were in precarious positions.

Joseph had watched as the number of suddenly indigent believers multiplied and realized God would have to supply food and money so they could eat. "The field." Now, where had that thought come from? He had purchased it as an investment soon after he moved from Cyprus. He then instinctively knew he needed to sell it. It had sold quickly and for a better price than Joseph had imagined.

Joseph's eyes refocused on the people around him. His hand instinctively patted the bag of coins tied to his belt, which responded with a muffled clink. He jiggled the bag once more before stepping to the front of the crowd and laying it on the ground before Peter. Peter's eyes widened as he reached into the bag and lifted the gold and silver coins before the congregation.

"Look how God has provided!" His voice boomed. "And by the hand of ... What is your name, Brother?"

"Joseph. Joseph from Cyprus," he replied slowly, not entirely comfortable being the focus of everyone's attention.

"No, not Joseph," the voice of another apostle called out. "You are Barnabas, truly the 'Son of Consolation.'"

Suddenly a stream of believers formed and began to present their own offerings. Others left only to return and add to the growing pile of coins, necklaces, bracelets, and rings. The Presence descended again as worship lifted from the lips of all.

Hours later, Joseph began working his way back through the throng of singers, almost missing the poorly dressed woman with gray hair and a warm smile who reached for his arm and spoke.

"Excuse me, Sister," he began, "I didn't quite catch what you said."

She smiled again. "I said, 'Thank you, Barnabas!'" And it stuck.

(Based on Acts 2–4)

Christian leadership is not a jacket you put on and take off depending on the situation that presents itself. Christian leadership is the outward expression of who you are as a person on the inside. It flows from your beliefs, values, and character. No matter what label you put on a tube of toothpaste, when you squeeze it, you will get what is inside the tube. If you want to be a leader, you must have the ingredients on the inside before you can manifest them on the outside.

The ingredients for leadership were evident in Barnabas' life. The same foundational principles that flowed from him and shaped both Paul and Mark continue to teach us today.

Start where you are. During the miraculous birth of the early church, thousands of people were making decisions to follow Christ. The apostles were overwhelmed with how to handle their success. During the previous three years, the twelve disciples had been a small, exclusive group under Jesus' direct supervision and care. Their needs had been few, and they had given little thought to the details of caring for the group. However, on the Day of Pentecost, the church grew by three thousand converts. Suddenly, there was a large group of new believers, many of them dependent on the apostles for their next meal.

> Christian leadership is the outward expression of who you are as a person on the inside.

Enter Barnabas! He may have been among the seventy whom Jesus sent out in Luke 10. Perhaps he was with the five hundred who watched in wonder as Jesus ascended into heaven. Possibly, he was with the 120 in the upper room when they were transformed by the Holy Spirit on the Day of Pentecost. Or Barnabas may have been among the three thousand who made the life-changing decision to make Jesus Christ their Messiah and Savior.

While Barnabas' past is unknown, he is a model for all who strive to become strong Christian leaders. The new church needed money to feed the new believers, and Barnabas had a field. Barnabas began with what he had. He decided to sell his property. "Joseph, who was also called by the apostles Barnabas (which means son of encouragement), a Levite, a native of Cyprus, sold a field that belonged to him and brought the money and laid it at the apostles' feet" (Acts 4:36–37).

When Jesus fed the five thousand, he didn't start with five loaves and two fishes. He didn't begin with a little boy whose mother made sure her son wouldn't go hungry. He began with His disciples. Andrew thought five loaves and a young boy's generosity were not enough to meet the need. Yet out of desperation and perhaps frustration, Andrew brought Jesus what he had.

Moses had a life-changing encounter with God. God called him to lead the nation of Israel out of Egypt, but Moses had many doubts and questions and asked, "How will they know you have sent me?" God responded, "What is that in your hand?" (Exodus 4:2). It was a shepherd's staff—really just a stick. But God used that stick to do miracles.

The key is to begin where you are. Don't wait until you have something you think is worth using; you will probably never be satisfied with what you have. Don't wait until you are better prepared; you will never be prepared enough. Don't wait until the time is "right"; there is no place like here and no time like the present. Start where you are with what you have.

On Sunday, December 16, 2000, at 10:42 a.m., as my wife, Terry, and I were worshiping about twelve rows back on the far-right side of a church in downtown Montevideo, Uruguay, God spoke to me. I fell to my knees, and He called me to plant ten churches in Uruguay.

I argued with the Lord because we were comfortably involved in Bible school ministry, and this was entirely new to us. There were others better prepared, more qualified, and more financially able to plant new churches. As I went back and forth in my mind, I could not imagine how it would work, but I became convinced of two things: God had called us, and we were to start where we were and use what we had!

Seek to serve. Barnabas took the payment from the sale of his field and gave it to the apostles. His selfless act is held in contrast to another gift, one from Ananias and his wife Sapphira. They also sold a piece of property but kept part of the money for themselves, laying the rest at the apostles' feet (Acts 5:1–2).

Ananias and Sapphira model a false leadership concept. Their goal was to be recognized for their gift. Recognition comes to many leaders for their accomplishments. However, recognition is just a by-product of service and a poor indicator of leadership ability.

Both Ananias and Sapphira died, not because they held back part of the proceeds from their property, but because they were so desirous of recognition that they were willing to lie to acquire it. They presented themselves as something they were not, and as a result they paid the ultimate price.

Barnabas' gift was an act of service. Service is meeting the need of another. It can be as simple as holding the door for an elderly couple to enter a building or as involved as dedicating your life to serving an unreached people group. At its best, service is a deeply held value that becomes a filter through which you view all aspects of life.

Service is the heartbeat of biblical leadership. Jesus said, "Whoever would be great among you must be your servant, and whoever would be first among you must be your slave, even as the Son of Man came not to be served but to serve" (Matthew 20:26–28). If you want to be a leader, serve.

It begins with looking away from yourself. Jesus' parable of the Good Samaritan is a story about service. Dr. Martin Luther King Jr. described the point of the parable like this: "The first question which the priest and the Levite asked was: 'If I stop to help this man, what will happen to me?' But ... the Good Samaritan reversed

23

the question: 'If I do not stop to help this man, what will happen to him?'"[1] Service is a matter of focus.

Harry, a national leader of a large denomination in the United States, was visiting us in Uruguay to speak at a pastors' convention. However, he spent one of his first days in bed because of problems with his throat. It was winter in North America, and he had cleared the snow from the walks of sixteen neighbors a few days before. He had gotten overheated in the cold and was paying the price. Harry's desire was to serve the Uruguayan pastors through the ministry of the Word. He was not looking for recognition for his selfless actions back in North America and would not have even mentioned his service were it not for his illness. His neighbors had a need, and Harry had a desire to serve.

Build people up. The early church gave Joseph a nickname. A nickname can be shorthand for one of a person's prominent characteristics. For example, someone who is tall may be called "Tree," while a person of diminutive stature may be called "Shorty." Joseph became Barnabas, the "son of encouragement" (Acts 4:36), because of something in his character that caused others to say, "You may be named Joseph, but you are an encourager, a Barnabas, to me."

Barnabas encouraged the apostles with his generosity. He encouraged a young, recently converted Saul who was trying to associate with the church that he had once persecuted in Acts 9. He later went to Tarsus to find and encourage an isolated Saul in Acts 11. Barnabas also took a rejected and discouraged Mark under his wing and sailed to Cyprus (Acts 15:39), once again demonstrating how he had earned his nickname.

> Encouragers focus on people more than just on tasks.

Encouragers focus on people more than just on tasks. The principal part of Jesus' passion occurred in the week between Palm and Resurrection Sundays, but He spent the majority of His earthly ministry pouring Himself into those who would establish His church. He ate what they ate and slept where they slept. Time and again, He placed them in situations that would challenge and stretch their faith. Everything focused on the day when He would ascend to His Father and leave them in charge of His church.

Encouragers multiply their efforts. What a leader can accomplish alone is not enough. The old saying, "If you want the job done right, do it yourself," becomes, "If you want to see amazing results, encourage others."

In the days after God gave us His vision, Terry and I prayed about how to plant ten Uruguayan churches. We realized we could not do it alone. The only church planting model I had known to that point was missionary centered. From the beginning, the missionary did everything from evangelizing to conducting services; from fund-raising to teaching Sunday school. After several months of hard work, a young pastor would be brought in to hopefully make the transition from missionary leadership to national leadership. However, we kept feeling there was another way—a way that would enable us to release the churches sooner, a way that would empower young pastors from the beginning of the new church, a way that would result in strong churches. Multiple churches, each led by young pastors known from the beginning, was the answer that kept coming back to us.

In 2003 we launched four churches and mentored four pastors. We birthed three more in 2006. After a return to the States and other ministry, we began the last three churches in 2012. In all three efforts, our focus was on the pastors. In all, ten pastors did the actual work of planting and pastoring. The churches grew, and there was no transition when Terry and I ended our involvement in the churches. We started where we were and built up the new pastors.

Leadership begins with a decision to start where you are with what you have. Your past successes or failures do not decide what you will do as much as your determination to begin. And serving others is the target that will direct your path. Service gives a reason to continue; it gives meaning to sacrifice. Building up others is the secret to successful leadership. Those who do the most to affect lives and encourage all with whom they come in contact will be remembered as effective biblical leaders.

Trust

When he (Saul) had come to Jerusalem, he attempted to join the disciples. And they were all afraid of him, ... But Barnabas

Barnabas smiled ruefully as he waited just outside the room where the apostles were meeting. He couldn't help but overhear as their voices penetrated the thin cloth that served as a door.

"How many more brothers and sisters can we afford to lose just to see if this madman can be trusted?" one asked.

Another remarked, "I was at Stephen's burial. And I watched helplessly as others were hauled off to prison, all because of Saul."

"Why did he leave for Damascus? Wasn't it to imprison more believers?"

"But what if Saul has changed? You know the Master would never turn him away."

Several now joined the debate. The pitch rose then quickly fell as one voice spoke above the others: "Has the Lord spoken to any of you? No? Then I say we wait."

"But what about Barnabas?" The voices hushed as the conversation continued.

Barnabas leaned back against the stone wall that separated him from the discussion. With the toe of his sandal, he shoved some dust over a black beetle that was trying to climb the wall. He watched as the insect repeatedly clawed its way through the barrier as Barnabas kicked more and more dirt over it.

He startled slightly when Peter pulled back the drape. "Brother Barnabas, we cannot agree to meet with young

Saul at this time." When Barnabas began to speak, Peter interrupted by raising his hand and adding, "However, we will not object if you still feel so strongly about seeing him. Talk to him. See if his story about seeing Jesus is true. Then let us know."

Barnabas nodded and turned to leave, but Peter continued, "And if you are committed to going, come in with us first so that we can pray with you."

(Based on Acts 9:26)

One of the fundamental building blocks of leadership is trust. Simply put, if I do not trust you, I will not follow you.

On a sunny afternoon long ago, I stood in the shallow end of our community pool, the water barely passing my ten-year-old knees. My three-year-old sister stood on the edge, fear written on her face. "Jump in, Ruthy!" I called, with my arms outstretched to catch her. She hesitated and stepped back, but I called to her again. After what seemed like an eternity, Ruthy crouched down, then launched herself into my arms. Her fear of the water was overruled by the confidence that her big brother wouldn't let her drown.

> If I do not trust you, I will not follow you.

Trust is confidence placed in the character of a friend, a spouse, or an authority. George MacDonald, a nineteenth-century Christian novelist whose works had a profound impact on many writers to follow, noted that being trusted is a greater compliment than being loved.[2]

The apostles had no confidence in young Saul. Perhaps memories of the deaths of Stephen and other believers were too fresh in their minds. They had lost friends to the wrath of this young Jewish leader who, just a short time before, had been "breathing threats and murder against the disciples of the Lord" (Acts 9:1). But they did trust Barnabas. He had earned the right to be heard by the leaders of the still-infant church.

Building trust is like erecting a brick house, laying one confidence-earning act or word upon another. Each trust-building brick is made up of four components: integrity, competence, transparency, and consistency.

Integrity. One of the most important characteristics of a well-built house is its integrity. A house with good integrity has a strong structure to keep it intact, protecting everything on the inside from harmful elements on the outside—from freezing cold, to searing heat, to the rain that can cause irreparable damage.

Jesus paints a powerful picture of building integrity in our lives:

> *Everyone then who hears these words of mine and does them will be like a wise man who built his house on the rock. And the rain fell, and the floods came, and the winds blew and beat on that house, but it did not fall, because it had been founded on the rock. And everyone who hears these words of mine and does not do them will be like a foolish man who built his house on the sand. And the rain fell, and the floods came, and the winds blew and beat against that house, and it fell, and great was the fall of it. (Matt. 7:24–27)*

Being a person of integrity means I will not allow the situations or temptations around me to influence or damage the core of uprightness and honesty that I maintain before the Lord.

Do you put this biblical principle into practice? Do those who know you best believe what you say? Do your family members trust that you will follow through on your promises? Do those who work with you know you will not repeat what they have told you in confidence? These are integrity issues that form the structure of who you are and guard your heart against outside influences.

Competence. Pam and Bill sat in surgeon Albert Smith's examination room looking at the certificates and photos that covered the walls. Beyond the expected framed degrees and achievements, the middle-aged couple studied the pictures of "Captain Smitty's" service in Iraq. The man who would remove the corn-kernel-sized tumor from Pam's left breast was a decorated combat surgeon. In the midst of their questions and fears, somehow the pictures of crossed Army campaign flags in front of dusty tents, armored personnel carriers, and the inside of a mobile surgical unit helped. They knew they could trust this man.

Competence says I can accomplish the tasks that I am assigned. I know what I am doing. It comes from studying and practicing to acquire a desired skill, whether it be doctoring the human body, preparing tax returns, or anything in between. It involves excellence (not perfection) and a sense of self-confidence.

Competence is a key component of trust. You may have integrity, but if you doubt your abilities or do not demonstrate excellence, I will struggle to trust you. Trust will come when I know you have the skills, ability, and confidence to do what is needed.

> Competence is a key component of trust.

Transparency. We once lived at the end of a road that led past several houses with large front windows. As we drove by in the evenings, my wife and I marveled at how the home owners often left the curtains open, giving us a full view of their front rooms. Whether they intended to be that transparent or not, their homes and lives were an open book for all to see.

Paul's second letter to the church in Corinth demonstrates his desire to be transparent with the church he had founded years before. "We have spoken freely to you, Corinthians; our heart is wide open" (2 Cor. 6:11). In other words, Paul was not hiding a secret agenda that he would eventually use against the Corinthian believers.

Transparency says the fewer secrets I maintain, the healthier and more effective I become. It's hard to keep secrets buried deep inside. The time, effort, and emotional energy required to maintain secrets leaves less in my tank for anything or anyone else. A simple, innocent question might bring me too close to painful truths that I don't want to slip out. When I choose to be transparent, the energy and thought that I previously spent in guarding those secrets can be directed in new ways.

Healthy transparency does not mean the absence of all confidentiality or privacy. On the contrary, transparency has limits that protect the private areas of my life. Houses generally are not made with just windows; they also have doors and walls to keep some areas private.

Healthy transparency ensures that I stay focused on the goals the Lord has laid out for me. A loving husband will share with his wife any circumstance that might affect their marriage. A caring wife will do the same. This kind of openness not only covers and protects a strong marital relationship but also forms the foundation for leadership.

Transparency says I do not disguise important goals and agendas; I am open about them. It means the pastor talks openly with the church leadership about his or her plans and aspirations for the group of believers he or she has been called to lead. When a leader conceals his or her ultimate goals and intentions from those under him or her, relationships and goals are endangered. A surprise birthday party is usually appreciated, but a surprise change in a church's or an organization's direction will often meet with confusion and perhaps opposition.

Consistency. Brick homes feature sharp corners and mortar joints that make for straight lines because bricks are consistent in their shape and size. The first brick is the same as the last, and that makes for a straight and strong house.

God is consistent. The theological word is *immutable* or *unchangeable*. The Psalmist puts it like this: "The counsel of the LORD stands forever, the plans of his heart to all generations" (Ps. 33:11). The writer of Hebrews declares that "Jesus Christ is the same yesterday and today and forever" (Heb. 13:8). This consistent God also demands consistency from His disciples, especially from His leaders.

Consistency says that others can count on me to be the same. While everyone faces the ups and downs and changes of daily life, consistent leaders will return to the baseline of dependable conduct that others recognize and respect.

Sam took a deep breath before knocking on his supervisor's door. He needed approval to authorize payment of an invoice but had received no response to his e-mail three days before. Unfortunately, this was a problem Sam was all too familiar with. He never knew how his boss would react. Some days brought laughter, stories, and good-natured ribbing; others brought dark looks, rebukes, and delays to important decisions. His supervisor's inconsistency was unsettling. Sam prayed silently for a good meeting, but the e-mail portended otherwise. "Come in," came the muffled voice through the door, but not with enough clarity to give Sam a sense of what awaited him. After another deep breath, he opened the door.

Consistency is not easy. The prophet Daniel faced a dangerous dilemma. He received an edict from King Darius to forego prayer to his God for thirty days. Trying to entrap him, Daniel's enemies counted on his unwavering devotion to God to trip him up. And the prophet proved true to his commitment. "He got down on his knees three times a day and prayed and gave thanks before his God, as he had done previously" (Dan. 6:10). Yet because of his consistency before God, Daniel was protected in the den of lions and was later honored by the king.

In fact, Daniel's story demonstrates the four components of trust working together. Daniel maintained his integrity by refusing to compromise his prayer life. Daniel was promoted in the court of his captors because of his recognized competence. He transparently opened the windows of his room so that all could see him pray. Finally, Daniel was consistent in his dedication to the Lord. Was it any surprise, then, that Daniel earned the respect and trust of kings?

Integrity. Competence. Transparency. Consistency. From the glimpses we get of him in Scripture, it seems Barnabas also demonstrated each of these qualities. He showed integrity in almost every aspect of his life, competence in his work at Antioch, transparency in his methods and agenda, and consistency throughout his ministry with Paul and later with Mark. Like Daniel, Barnabas' solid character established him as a leader whom others could respect and trust.

Make it a goal to be trustworthy. Maintain your integrity. Hone your skills to develop competence. Be open and avoid secrets from those who count on you. Remain consistent in your dealings. In this way, you will build strong, trusting relationships, both with those you lead and with those who lead you.

Vision

Barnabas watched as Saul shifted his weight uneasily on the stool in the corner of the small room. The afternoon sun peeked through the closed windows and door, adding to the weak light that came from the small oil lamps hanging near the walls. The smoke from the lamps hung in the air. After approaching Saul at the well and introducing himself, Barnabas had brought the young Pharisee to this dark room, trying to keep their meeting as secret as possible.

Barnabas smiled nervously and cleared his throat. "I've heard of your encounter with the Lord from others," he said, "but could you tell me in your own words what happened on the road to Damascus?"

Saul's eyes lit up, and he leaned forward. Words began to pour like a waterfall from his heart, expressing his passion to protect what he thought was the true worship of God, the plaguing questions that came after seeing Stephen's expression when he forgave those who took his life, and then the undeniable reality that surrounded Saul's own encounter with Jesus Christ.

Barnabas asked, "So you knew it was Jesus when He first spoke to you, then?"

Saul's voice faltered for the first time, and his eyes clouded. "I guess I was more afraid that it was Him. I mean, I can't even tell you how many believers are dead because of me ..." His voice trailed away to almost a whisper.

Barnabas stood quietly as one, then another tear trickled down Saul's cheek and into his beard. He stepped over to the former persecutor and placed a hand on his shoulder. "Saul, the Master taught us about the power of forgiveness. I knew Stephen. Many of those whom you ... who are now with the Lord were friends of mine. I can see that Jesus has forgiven you. I think you need to hear that I forgive you as well."

Saul's head lowered, and his shoulders drooped as he heaved a long sigh. While Barnabas watched the young man work through his feelings, something happened deep inside his own spirit. It was like the morning sun crossing a threshold, chasing away the night's shadows. He saw that God's hand was on Saul. He saw that God was going to use Saul to build His church. And Barnabas knew that God was calling him to help young Saul become a chosen instrument to build that church.

Barnabas walked over to the window and opened it wide. He looked out to the street and called over his shoulder, "Come with me, Brother Saul. It's time you meet Peter and your other brothers and sisters in Christ."

(Based on Acts 9:26–27)

We have no actual record of Barnabas' and Saul's first meeting. At some point, Barnabas came face to face with the former persecutor of the church and saw something that grabbed his attention, sparking a relationship that would change both men's lives.

Vision is the ability to look past the obvious, to see what might be. Paraphrasing a character in a George Bernard Shaw play, the late US senator Robert F. Kennedy said, "Some men see things as they are and say, why; I dream things that never were and say, why not."[3] Vision is a cornerstone of great leadership.

Yet vision is often a lonely perspective. Those around you will question you, doubting the possibilities you see as realities. They will give you a thousand reasons to question what you see. In fact, many good, honest people will never see what you see. Automotive pioneer Henry Ford saw a better way to build cars through the

> Vision is the ability to look past the obvious, to see what might be.

assembly-line process when others were still handcrafting each individual vehicle. The Wright brothers saw people flying and built the first working airplane when others said it was impossible. To a nation that had divided black and white people into two unequal groups, US civil rights leader Martin Luther King Jr. spoke of his dream of white and black children playing together.

Vision is the hallmark of great leadership, but it is not automatic.

Vision often begins with an unsettledness with things as they are, whether bad or good. The circumstances don't matter as much as the sense that they could be different. The metal cans so common in the food industry today were first invented in 1810 to transport food to Napoleon's armies in the field. The first cans were made of iron, often outweighed the food they contained, and had to be opened with a hammer and chisel. In 1846 metal became thinner, and special molds were invented. In 1858 the first can opener, which looked like a bayonet and sickle, made its appearance; the can opener that most of us know today came out in 1870.[4] Today, many cans have a pull tab, so no can opener is needed. Each step in the evolution of the can came when someone became unsettled with what was and began thinking of what could be.

Barnabas was never content with the way things were. It was a characteristic of his ministry. He saw the chasm between the apparently repentant Saul and the cautious body of believers, and he introduced the young Christian to the leadership of the early church. We see Barnabas' vision again when he left Antioch to look for Saul in Tarsus and later when he left Paul to take Mark under his wing. Each time it would have been far easier to stay with the known, the comfortable, and the acceptable.

My first experience with unsettledness began with a certificate on the wall of the church we attended in Ohio. It was the church's pledge to give one thousand dollars by the end of the year for gospel literature to be used overseas, and it called to me every time I entered the building. Only a handful of believers attended that church at the time, and giving a thousand dollars seemed like an impossibility. Weeks went by, and nothing happened. I mentioned the commitment to the women's group in the church and talked about the need during prayer meetings. Surely, someone would catch the vision to raise the funds.

I finally realized that someone *had* caught the vision—me! I talked to Terry and then to the pastor about taking donations of used goods for a community garage sale. Soon volunteers were picking up used lawn mowers, washing machines, leather goods, and even a set of large speakers cased in mahogany panels— enough goods to fill the parking lot across from the county courthouse. The sale brought in most of the needed money, and the church made up what was lacking. God showed Himself faithful to bless the efforts of our small congregation, and He laid a foundation in my life of turning my unsettledness into His provision.

Vision faces reality. Saul had persecuted the church. Barnabas didn't hide or make excuses for Saul's past. He faced it head on.

In the Old Testament, Nehemiah had a vision for rebuilding the walls of Jerusalem. Nehemiah 2 tells of his inspecting the brokendown walls late at night, stepping over the jumbled piles of rocks that had once defended a proud city. He wanted to know the extent of the challenges that lay ahead.

In the latter part of the 1800s, Frenchman Ferdinand de Lesseps had a vision of building a sea-level canal across the Isthmus of Panama. Besides the health risks of malaria and yellow fever, crossing the Culebra (Snake) mountain range presented a daunting challenge. French engineers recommended a system of locks to raise ships over the mountains, but Lesseps insisted on a sea-level canal. As a result, the excavation of the Culebra Cut was plagued by landslides that destroyed equipment and slowed progress, while the heat and disease took thousands of lives, eventually bankrupting Lesseps' company. Lesseps refused to face reality and suffered the consequences. In contrast, the US canal effort focused on wiping out the diseases and then building a lock-based canal that lifted ships over the Culebra mountain range—just as the French engineers had suggested years earlier. Because the US canal effort faced and overcame the challenges, today millions of tons of cargo are taken every year across the fifty-one-mile passage, saving ships the eighteen-thousand-mile trip around South America.[5]

A challenge that is denied is rarely defeated and does not demonstrate great vision. Denied challenges will destroy vision and visionaries. Vision recognizes reality. Vision *faces* reality.

> A challenge that is denied is rarely defeated and does not demonstrate great vision.

One night several years ago, the look on Terry's face told me she was struggling to tell me something. We had been married for nine years and were in our hotel room in Columbus, Ohio, during a couples' retreat for ministers. The speaker had powerfully ministered on intimacy and transparency. Finally, she managed to say, "I was abused when I was a child."

Those words began a process for us that has shaped our lives and ministry. Our healing journey has been both painful and powerful. What Satan intended to use to destroy her life, God turned into a blessing as Terry faced her reality and later shared her testimony. In fact, at least two young women are in ministry today in Uruguay as a result of hearing Terry's story. Each shared a similar story, each faced her own reality, and each went through her own healing process. And facing and dealing with Terry's reality sparked my interest in Barnabas, the "son of consolation."

Vision looks for possibilities. "Maybe he hasn't really changed." Barnabas had to have considered that thought as he pondered meeting with the former persecutor. But he didn't stop there. The possibility that "then again, maybe he *has* changed" opened the door for Saul to become the apostle Paul and everything that lay ahead.

Possibility thinking, out-of-the-box thinking, and brainstorming all are synonyms for creatively considering new options for a course of action. Jesus spent three years teaching His disciples to look for the possibilities. He inspired Peter to consider the possibility of walking on water. He taught Andrew to look for the possibilities in two little fish and five small loaves.

A young missionary couple were preparing to purchase their first vehicle in their adopted country. Based on our twenty years of experience, we warned them, "Buying a car overseas is different than buying one in the United States. Dealerships don't allow test drives—they never have and never will." Fortunately, the young couple did not heed our words. They asked the dealership and were soon test driving a model similar to the car they later ordered. Their philosophy of "It never hurts to ask"—their possibility thinking—was rewarded.

The question *why not?* gives birth to creativity. The door that has always been locked may one day surprise you and open.

Vision inspires those around you. Winston Churchill was a rock-solid bastion of leadership. For nearly five years, he stood firm as waves of Nazi attacks filled the oceans and skies around Britain until she and her allies turned the tide of war. One story tells of Churchill's visit to England's coal miners to increase production and keep the war effort moving forward.

> *At the end of his presentation he asked them to picture in their minds a parade which he knew would be held in Picadilly Circus after the war. First, he said, would come the sailors who had kept the vital sea lanes open. Then would come the soldiers who had come home from Dunkirk and then gone on to defeat Rommel in Africa. Then would come the pilots who had driven the Luftwaffe from the sky. "Last of all, he said, would come a long line of sweat-stained, soot-streaked men in miner's caps. Someone would cry from the crowd, 'And where were you during the critical days of our struggle?' And from ten thousand throats would come the answer, 'We were deep in the earth with our faces to the coal.'"*[6]

Churchill's vision inspired not only these coal miners but also the young and old in Great Britain and around the world to achieve one of the greatest economic and military victories in history.

Jesus' vision of what His Father had called Him to do caught fire in the lives of His disciples. In turn, they gave their own lives for the good news that Jesus had defeated sin through His death and resurrection.

Barnabas' vision inspired the apostles in Jerusalem to accept Saul as a brother. Later, his vision led him to take Saul and then

Mark under his wing, impacting both young men during the formative years of their ministries.

Let your vision become your passion. Over the years, many have shared with me their dreams and visions of what they have felt God wanted them to do. I remember those who spoke with passion—the ones who convinced me that nothing would keep them from fulfilling their vision. Your passion will carry you through the early days of inexperience and mistakes, and it will inspire those around you.

> Your passion will carry you through the early days of inexperience and mistakes

Learn to express your vision in a few concise words. Your listeners will not understand what you want to do if you cannot communicate it in a simple, memorable way. In our denomination, missionaries raise support for their ministries by sharing their vision of what God has called them to do. They hope that both churches and individuals will be inspired to join them with prayer and financial support. When Terry and I were just starting to raise support, one pastor required missionaries to share their calling with his congregation in seven minutes or less. I will never forget standing nervously before that crowd, sharing as succinctly as possible how God had called Terry and me to minister in Uruguay. I stepped down from the platform just before the deadline, and the church joined our growing family of supporters. This pastor did us a great service because he forced us to boil down our presentation without losing the passion we felt so deeply. That exercise has helped me time and again in hundreds of churches around the world.

Barnabas saw things that others could or would not see. His vision began with a discontent for the way things were. He never settled for what was comfortable or acceptable but reached for the unknown. He was not afraid to face stark realities. Yet, with both Saul and Mark, he looked beyond past failures to envision future possibilities, and his vision inspired others to do the same.

Barnabas' vision powerfully impacted the people around him. So what do you see?

Failure

The Hellenists... were seeking to kill him (Saul).
And when the brothers learned this, they brought him
down to Caesarea and sent him off to Tarsus

"Could I have been wrong about him, Lord?" Silence answered Barnabas' unspoken prayer, but he already knew the answer. There had been no mistake about Saul's conversion. There had been no mistake about Saul's zeal for the gospel of Jesus Christ. Barnabas had seen that from the beginning. But Saul's attempts to share the good news of great joy had quickly descended into bitter debates focused on forcing Jews to accept Jesus as the Messiah.

Barnabas looked down the hill toward the harbor then over to his left at Saul. The young man's eyes were downcast, and his face mirrored the turmoil in his soul. Andrew and John walked just ahead. Every so often, John glanced over his shoulder, his eyes filled with concern. The only sound was the dull thud of sandals on the dirt road that led to the port of Caesarea.

Sailors were loading the Gaulus *with a shipment of olive oil destined for Tarsus. The shipmaster confirmed that his boat was scheduled to leave with the morning's tide and that there was room for another passenger. The group quickly worked out and paid the price of Saul's passage.*

It seemed the Spirit was still with them. Barnabas marveled at how everything had fallen into place over the past week. The apostles had acted quickly to deal with Saul. And from the moment Saul was secreted out of Jerusalem, nothing more had been heard from the Grecian Jews who had been viciously plotting Saul's death.

Barnabas watched dejectedly as Saul walked up the gang-plank with his small bundle of possessions and turned to look back at those who were sending him home. He didn't smile or wave. He just threw a questioning look at the people whom he had persecuted, then wholeheartedly joined, and who now silently waited at the dock just long enough to ensure that he didn't jump ship before it embarked.

As the lines were cast off and the ship slowly moved into the current, Barnabas wondered silently, "What are You doing, Lord?" There was so much promise in this young man, yet disaster seemed to follow him wherever he went. Still, Barnabas was convinced that God would find a way for Saul to fulfill the words spoken over him: "a chosen instrument of mine to carry my name before the Gentiles and kings."

(Based on Acts 9:28–30)

Those who believe that failure is not an option rarely venture beyond the boundaries of their own comfort zones. Yet those who take risks realize that sooner or later they will experience some type of failure. Saul failed in his early attempt to become a Christian leader. In a sense, Barnabas failed as well. Saul was ministering in the church because Barnabas "cosigned" for him, putting his own reputation and the trust he had earned with the apostles on the line.

"I think I am doing more harm than good," I told Terry as I wearily came through the front door of our home after a long day. We were in our first missionary term and in charge of the local Bible school, and I was dealing with a discipline problem with one of our very first residential students. He was facing suspension.

> Those who believe that failure is not an option rarely venture beyond the boundaries of their own comfort zones.

While I thought I had handled the initial situation well, I really didn't understand the Uruguayan students' culture. When his fellow students asked me what had happened, I explained that I couldn't share the details of the discipline with them. However, those seven students were like a family and intensely felt the suspension of their friend. I didn't understand that they needed me to walk them through the process of their fellow student leaving the Bible school. I thought they were trying to pry. As a result, I almost lost an entire class when they threatened to walk out.

That evening I threw myself on my bed and covered my face with a pillow, hot tears running down my cheeks. That's when I heard the Lord speak to my heart. "Could you offer what you have done as an offering to Me?" How could I lift up my failure to the Lord? It was like presenting God a blind lamb with a broken leg. Yet three times He asked till I finally raised my cupped hands as an offering to Him.

Nothing changed, at least not immediately. Tensions continued high, casting a shadow over everything we did until the end of the school year. However, that moment became a white-hot forge in my life that melted much of my pride and formed the foundation for many of the blessings we have experienced in our ministry over the years.

Barnabas had taken a risk in endorsing Saul, and it seemed to have failed. Yet, despite how it looked at the moment, he had to trust that God would somehow work Saul's failure and misguided zeal for good.

These three principles may help to change your perspective on failure.

1 **Don't mistake unfulfilled expectations for failures.** To most of the Jewish leadership of New Testament times, Jesus was a failed Messiah. Regardless of His miracles and teaching, Jesus did not fulfill their expectations for the Messiah—the one who was to reestablish the kingdom of David and end the domination of their Roman occupiers.

We see the same concept throughout the Bible. The last portion of Hebrews 11 contains a list of the "failed" heroes of the faith.

Others suffered mocking and flogging, and even chains and im-prisonment. They were stoned, they were sawn in two, they were killed with the sword. They went about in skins of sheep and goats, destitute, afflicted, mistreated—of whom the world was not wor-

thy—wandering about in deserts and mountains, and in dens and caves of the earth. (vv. 36–38)

These saints were honored for their faithfulness but never experienced what most would consider to be success. God's standard of success and failure is far different from ours.

George, a successful Christian businessman, captured a vision for reaching Uruguay. He was instrumental in sponsoring several evangelistic outreaches throughout the country and helped with the purchase of many church properties. Yet George often came to me after an evangelistic outreach or a church plant very disappointed. It was not what he had imagined. Many people had made life-changing commitments to Christ. Others had received divine healing, and marriages had been restored. But George was expecting thousands to be converted, the dead to be raised, and so much more. My answer was always the same: "Just look, George, at what God *has* done here." Over time, we have witnessed the long-term results of George's investment in the tiny Latin American country—results that have gone far beyond what George first pictured.

2 Don't let failure define you. A wise man once said, "Don't build your shrine on the mountaintops, and don't dig your grave in the valleys." Neither the high nor the low moments occupy the majority of our lives, and they do not define who we are. Abraham Lincoln's list of failures far outnumbered his successes: In 1832 he was defeated for state legislature. He failed in business in 1833 and was defeated in elections for public office in 1838, 1843, 1848, 1854, 1856, and 1858. But he refused to let those defeats define him. In 1860, just two years after his latest defeat, Lincoln was elected as the sixteenth president of the United States, best known for leading America through the dark years of the Civil War.

Paul paints an amazing contrast in the book of Romans: "As it is written, 'For your sake we are being killed all the day long; we are regarded as sheep to be slaughtered.' No, in all these things we are more than conquerors through him who loved us" (Rom. 8:36–37). In other words, you can choose to allow past failures to tell you who you are. Or you can choose another path, one that defines who you are by the Word of God: more than a conqueror.

When you define yourself by God's Word, failures become detours, setbacks, and training grounds that help determine the person God wants you to be in His kingdom. One of my wife's favorite passages in the Bible is Psalm 129. Verse 3 tells us, "The plowers plowed upon my back: they made long their furrows. (But) the Lord is righteous; he has cut the cords of the wicked." The image that comes to my mind is of a horse pulling a heavy plow of failure that cuts deep into my heart. But then God cuts the reins and harness attached to that plow. He plants seed of healing in those furrows. And the harvest is always much more than just for me.

> When you define yourself by God's Word, failures become detours, setbacks, and training grounds that help determine the person God wants you to be

3 Don't let failure become the last chapter of your story. I stood just outside the entrance of the campaign tent listening to our young church planter, Sergio, pour out his heart. Sergio was just finishing Bible school training, and the new outreach was only a few weeks old. Yet he was already facing a crisis that threatened everything we had prayed and worked so hard for.

The week before, a middle-aged father had crossed the busy highway beside our newly purchased property to attend the evangelistic services. He seemed very excited and brought his sixteen-year-old daughter with him the following night. But just days later came the awful report that the father had killed his wife before taking his life with a pistol. Relatives had taken the girl.

Sergio was devastated. The evangelist who was ministering nightly in the campaign services told our young pastor that the tragedy was his fault. He said that somehow Sergio should have foreseen and prevented this savage attack. Of course, the evangelist was wrong. This was an attack from Satan designed to destroy a family and a new church plant all in one blow. But to Sergio, it felt like a failure. We talked and prayed together before he returned to the service that was just beginning. The entire neighborhood was aware of what had happened and was watching for our response.

We were tempted to move the campaign or even cancel services for a time. In the end, we decided not to allow the enemy to detour the direction that we felt so strongly from the Lord. The campaign continued, and today *La Casa de Alabanza* (House of Praise) church continues to reach the surrounding community with the good news of Jesus Christ.

Barnabas did not allow Saul's failure to be the last chapter in their relationship. Saul did not allow it either. Rather, the Holy Spirit used Barnabas to walk alongside Saul through the process that led him into effective and powerful ministry.

The crucifixion of Jesus brought failures on the part of His followers. Peter denied Him. Thomas refused to believe Jesus was risen till he personally touched the nail prints in His hands and the spear cut in His side. All of them scattered like lost sheep. Yet all except Judas came back. Judas' act of betrayal became the final chapter that ended with taking his own life. God did not destine you to close the book of your life with a failure.

> After every failure comes the decision of what to do next.

After every failure comes the decision of what to do next. A pastor's moral failure brings the choice of going through the painful restoration process or leaving ministry for something else. An unexpected pregnancy in a young teen brings the unavoidable decision of whether to abort, give the baby up for adoption, or keep the baby. (It is far too easy to take the life of an unborn baby in our culture. Many young women's lives have been devastated by a decision to abort.) Whatever the situation, God has a solution. Your or another's failure does not have to be the ending chapter in your life. Allow the Holy Spirit to start a new chapter.

Barnabas had to face any unfulfilled expectations he may have had of the young Saul. But Barnabas refused to let that apparent failure define him or his ministry. He was still known as the "son of encouragement," not for what some may have considered a mistake. Barnabas did not allow this perceived failure to change who he was or to become the last chapter of his life.

What about the failures in your life? Are you avoiding the pain of facing them? Has your life fallen short of your expectations? Don't let failure define who you are. Let Jesus Christ speak to you through His Word. Don't ignore your mistakes, but don't let them have the last word. Let them be your teachers for the future. Ask God to help you begin a new chapter. You may be amazed at how it turns out!

Authority

*Those who were scattered because of the persecution...
traveled as far as Phoenicia and Cyprus and Antioch... The church
in Jerusalem... sent Barnabas to Antioch*

Barnabas' eyes opened again in the darkness of the unfamiliar house, sleep still eluding him. He could hear a light snore coming from the brother who had taken him in. What was his name? Lucius; yes, it was Lucius. The apostles had told Barnabas that Lucius and his wife would feed him and give him a place to sleep, even though it meant bedding their girls in a corner to give the young leader a place to lay his head.

Across the room, a little one called out softly in the night, and Barnabas heard the rustle of her mother's hand reaching out to comfort the small girl. The mother's low voice whispered, "Shush, my love, you will wake the man of God." Barnabas frowned to himself. First the believers called him Barnabas, and now man of God? He knew all his doubts and weaknesses even if others did not see them.

Barnabas rolled on his side, willing his body to relax. Sleep had been hard to come by ever since he had accepted the apostles' request to leave Jerusalem and lead the group of believers in Antioch. That had been more than two weeks ago. Barnabas had replayed his conversation with Peter and James almost daily as he zigzagged his way north through Samaria and Galilee, skirting Mount Carmel, then Mount Lebanon, following many of the same paths Jesus had walked.

"You really feel that I can do this?" Barnabas' gaze had shifted back and forth between the two apostles.

James had smiled. "Brother Barnabas, we have prayed long and hard about who would be best to guide these new be-

lievers." *Peter had nodded in agreement as James continued, "Your name came up over and over again."*

Barnabas wasn't so sure, but he didn't want to betray their trust in him. Still, each long day on the road had brought new questions and doubts. These were God's chosen leaders. But how well did they know what Barnabas was capable of doing?

Someone on the other side of the room coughed, then sighed. Barnabas wondered what the apostles were doing back home. They were probably huddled together, praying. Good idea. Maybe praying silently for each of the brothers would help put him to sleep.

"Father, I lift Brother James to You. Lord, You know he is much more qualified to take charge of the flock of new believers here." He paused, knowing that the apostles were trying to stay together, at least for now. "Lord, what am I going to do? There are so many who have no teaching, no foundation I can build upon." He paused again. Clearly, something amazing had been happening as one after another, Jew and Gentile alike—no one really knew how many—had joyfully confessed Jesus Christ as the Messiah. Somebody needed to walk alongside these new brothers and sisters. Someone needed to disciple them. Someone ... "Ok, ok, Father! I'm here. I will do what I can. I will love them just as You love me. But, Lord, for tonight, please just help me get some sleep!"

Suddenly, as if he had just dropped a long-carried weight, Barnabas' muscles relaxed, and his eyes grew heavy. Now, who was next to be prayed for? He never remembered.

(Based on Acts 11:19–22)

Working with and submitting yourself to the authority God has placed over you is a fundamental part of biblical leadership. When you first enter ministry, there is so much to learn. You are more open to suggestions and guidance. But as the years pass by, you begin to see the human frailties and faults of those who serve in leadership over you. You see that those in authority are not infallible, and you may even have to experience the results of their mistakes. It can become more difficult to accede to the guidance of imperfect leaders. And yet they are entrusted with decisions that affect all those who serve with them. Barnabas models the answer to this dilemma for all of us.

Obedience, the outward evidence. At this point in his ministry, Barnabas was a trusted leader. In the apostles' minds, Barnabas was the ideal choice to guide the new and growing group of Christians in the city of Antioch. But how did Barnabas feel about moving so far from everything and everyone he knew to help this group of young believers? Antioch was a major Roman city of approximately 500,000 inhabitants. It was a different country, a different culture, a completely different situation. Just traveling from Jerusalem to Antioch would have taken approximately eighteen days. What if the apostles were mistaken in their request?

Barnabas' actions speak of his feelings. He obeyed the apostles' request and moved to Antioch. Yielding to direction from leadership is founded on the biblical principle of obedience, first to God, then to established authority. Jesus asked His followers, "Why do you call me 'Lord, Lord,' and not do what I tell you?" (Luke 6:46). In other words, "How can you call Me Lord, Savior, and Master if you don't obey what I tell you to do? If you are My follower, you will do what I ask you to do." Peter takes this principle further by including earthly authority. He tells us to be subject for the Lord's sake to every human institution and, moreover, to be subject to our leaders with "all respect, not only to the good and gentle but also to the unjust" (1 Pet. 2:13–18).

Kendall and Starla Bridges have written a powerful book, *Better Marriage: Against All Odds*, in which they open their hearts about Kendall's devastating moral failure while pastoring in Houston, Texas. Beyond all the levels of healing that Kendall and Starla needed in their relationship, Kendall was determined to walk through the rigorous restoration process for his ministry.

> *I'm not going to lie; This was very hard. In the days following my confession, we were faced with the decision of what to do now. I had resigned from my church, but now we had to face whatever type of disciplinary action or process I was willing to accept. It was my only hope of ever being involved in ministry again.*[7]

For Kendall that meant submitting to weekly meetings with a supervising pastor, monthly meetings with an area leader, bimonthly meetings with the Ministerial Relations Committee, counseling sessions, and monthly reports "which entailed my daily devotional habits and personal journaling." On top of everything, he was to have no ministry for one year and another year of sporadic ministry with the permission of those he was accountable to.

Today, Kendall and Starla are the lead pastors of Freedom Church in Carrollton, Texas, which over two thousand people call their church home. The restoration miracle the Bridges are living out came about through love and forgiveness and because of their submission to the authority God had placed over them.

> One of the hardest things you will do is yield to a person or situation that appears wrong or unjust in your eyes.

It's not always easy to submit to authority. Other sources offered Kendall options of a three-month or a six-month-to-a-year restoration process, but he chose the longer and harder path. In the end, his choice to submit to the longer path toward restoration earned the trust not only of his wife but also of those in authority over him, and now of his congregation.

Jesus submitted Himself to the authority of His earthly parents (Luke 2:51), to John's baptism (Matt. 3:13), to the temple authority by paying the temple tax (Matt. 17:27), but most importantly to the will of His heavenly Father. "For I have come down from heaven, not to do my own will but the will of him who sent me" (John 6:38). That obedient submission purchased our salvation when Jesus "humbled himself by becoming obedient to the point of death, even death on a cross" (Phil. 2:8).

Probably one of the hardest things you will do is yield to a person or situation that appears wrong or unjust in your eyes. It's not always easy to submit to authority. Leaders don't always get it right. Their motives are just as fallible as yours or mine. Their mistakes during your most vulnerable moments will tempt you to step out from under their biblical authority. But in the end, it's not about what they do or say; it's about your heart.

Are there moments when you must resist authority? Absolutely! Our ultimate authority is the Word of God. Any suggestion or mandate that we violate the Word is in itself outside biblical authority. When the Jewish leaders ordered the apostles not to preach Jesus, the apostles' response was, "We must obey God rather than men!" (Acts 5:29). However, you should never use that Scripture verse as an excuse to ignore or disobey those placed in biblical authority over you just because you disagree with the direction you have been given.

Attitude, the inward evidence. Obedience with a bad attitude can be as bad as disobedience, sometimes worse. A bad attitude can sink the best efforts. A good attitude can lift the worst situation.

Barnabas revealed his attitude about his new assignment in Antioch. When "he came and saw the grace of God, he was glad, and he exhorted them all to remain faithful to the Lord with steadfast purpose" (Acts 11: 23). In other words, Barnabas did not look at his new assignment as a burdensome task but rejoiced in his heart. What a great attitude!

Our youngest, Brianne, is an incredible young Christian woman and leader in her local church. Those leadership skills come in part from a very strong will that would occasionally require attention when she was growing up. Her mother and I used a form of time-out to deal with those moments. Once, we sent our three-and-a-half-year-old to her room until her "attitude was appropriate." She marched in, slamming the door shut, only to fling it open a few minutes later. She yelled out, "I'm not 'appopiate' yet!" struggling greatly with that big word. Then she slammed the door shut again. But we got the message, and Dad made her open and shut the door correctly as we all waited for her attitude to change. It did.

> Obedience with a bad attitude can be as bad as disobedience, sometimes worse.

Your attitude toward an assigned task will always color the result. It can show up in the tone of your response to a question, the attention you pay to the concerns of another, or something as simple as your eye contact. I boarded a return flight from an overseas trip exhausted from eleven days of heavy ministry and soon fell asleep, missing supper. Sometime later, the flight attendant caught me with my eyes open, remembered that I had not eaten, and brought me some orange juice. A few hours later, she checked on me again. Regardless of her own tiredness from working a long overnight flight, the woman demonstrated her attitude toward her customers. As I exited the aircraft, I took joy in handing her an airline-issued coupon for excellent service. It was the first time I had given one out, but I doubt it was the first time she had received one. Her positive attitude made a huge difference to a weary traveler.

Bringing your attitude in line with your obedience takes ministry to an entirely new level. Paul speaks about it in Romans, pairing acts of ministry with empowering attitudes: "The one who contributes, in generosity; the one who leads, with zeal; the one who does acts of mercy, with cheerfulness" (Rom. 12:8). In other words, giving that comes from a generous attitude, leadership that is based in enthusiasm, and mercy that is saturated with joy reflect the heart of God. You are not obligated to be generous, to be a leader, or to be a mercy giver. You have the tremendous honor of doing so, and that attitude will impact everyone around you.

One of the most important attitudes you can manifest to others is humility. Humility speaks of our relationship to the Lord. We depend on Him for everything, not on ourselves. Jesus teaches this in the Lord's Prayer: "Give us today our daily bread ... forgive us our debts ... lead us not into temptation" (Matt. 6:10–12). A young child is taught to humbly accept his or her parents' authority, recognizing that he or she is dependent on them. In the same way, we humbly accept God's authority, knowing that we are dependent on Him.

In our relationship with others, humility calls us to service. John and James' mother asked Jesus to place her sons beside Him in His kingdom, a position over the other disciples. Jesus responded,

You know that the rulers of the Gentiles lord it over them, and their great ones exercise authority over them. It shall not be so among you. But whoever would be great among you must be your servant, and whoever would be first among you must be your slave, even as

the Son of Man came not to be served but to serve, and to give his life as a ransom for many. (Matt. 20:25–28)

I once asked an eighty-year-old, still very active missionary, "How is humility reflected in our daily lives as leaders?" His answer surprised me: "It's the willingness to accept the ministry of others." In other words, the humble leader allows others to speak into his or her life words of encouragement, words of guidance, and at times words of correction. Humility says that I do not have all the answers and that God often uses the wisdom of others to help guide my life.

Barnabas submitted to the authority of the apostles. He showed both the outer evidence of obedience and submission to their request and the inner evidence of a great attitude toward his ministry assignment. What was the result? "A great many people were added to the Lord" (Acts 11:24). The church grew! Does your attitude lift or sink those around you? Let Barnabas' example lift or perhaps change you!

Spirituality

For he (Barnabas) was a good man, full of the Holy Spirit and of faith

Barnabas quickly covered his mouth to stifle a yawn. The sun had gone down hours before, and the worship and teaching time had long ago ended. Adrenaline had fueled the first hour of prayer for the line of sick and needy who continued to press forward for his touch. Now his back protested as he bent down to listen to the needs of a very short Jewish believer who leaned on a tall staff.

As he began to pray, she half released, half tossed her staff. It bounced off one of the other brothers who was praying for her before rattling down to the stone floor. Her hands shot up and began to wave around. "It's gone! It's gone!" she shouted before grabbing the robe of the same young man she had just hit with her staff and dancing around. Barnabas took a step back to avoid a collision, stretched his back, and smiled. He hadn't really understood what the woman had mumbled in his ear over the noise of the other praying believers. Whatever it was, God had taken care of it!

Afterward, Barnabas sat down with a dozen of his new friends here in Antioch to share a late supper. Any later and it would have been an early breakfast. As they waited for the hosts to serve the simple meal of bread and dates, they began to share stories of the salvations, healings, and miracles the Lord had done in their lives. Leaning back against the wall, Barnabas tried to follow the low but joyous conversations, but his eyes grew heavier by the second. His chin dropped to his chest, and he fell fast asleep.

No one noticed until he failed to reach for the bread that was being passed to him. The young man to his left who

was offering the bread nudged his neighbor, who nudged another, and so on till all conversation died away. Not wanting to disturb this man whom they all respected, each one silently stood, grabbed handfuls of food, and went outside. The host draped his own cloak over the apostle's body and then put out the lamps one by one, except the last one by the doorway. "That's just in case he wakes before dawn," he explained to his wife quietly. "We don't want him to stumble in the dark."

(Based on Acts 11:24)

The first description of Barnabas' character came in the form of his nickname. He was also called a good man because of his selfless obedience and good attitude in taking charge of the spiritual care of the believers in Antioch. Luke now fills in more detail about Barnabas: He was "full of the Holy Spirit and of faith." Luke had used the same description to introduce the first Christian martyr, Stephen, in Acts 6. These were significant words of high praise.

Full of the Holy Spirit. Many leadership books, seminars, blogs, and studies are written or conducted without considering this all-important element. Secular leadership is a closed circle that precludes any input outside the human leadership/influence/coaching world. But biblical leadership depends upon the Holy Spirit. It is an open circle with a place for the Holy Spirit's direction.

> Biblical leadership is an open circle with a place for the Holy Spirit's direction.

In the first chapter of Acts, Jesus commanded His followers to take the gospel to the world but then told them to wait until they were empowered by the Holy Spirit. Human wisdom and effort were not enough to accomplish the task of reaching the world. Barnabas and Saul began their pioneering missionary journey after they received a prophetic word from the Holy Spirit. Acts 16 describes how Paul was directed by the Holy Spirit away from Turkey and into Greece during his missionary journey.

I first felt the specific guidance of the Holy Spirit when I was just sixteen years old. On a Sunday morning at the altar area in my home church, I heard the voice of the Lord calling me to dedicate my life to His service. The second came nineteen years later when I heard His voice inside my mind, saying, "Go!"—the encounter that led Terry and me to begin our missionary career. That one word was like the seed of a rose falling into my heart, instantly blooming into a thorny flower. There was nothing so sweet as following that voice and nothing so painful as leaving everything behind to do so. Then eleven years later, the voice came to me that Sunday morning during worship at a church in Montevideo, leading us to begin a new ministry of planting churches.

Once you open your mind to the leading of the Holy Spirit, you need to learn how to recognize His voice. Everyone entertains thoughts and feelings that come from all kinds of sources. My principles and values are mostly from my parents and come to me in the form of ideas and motivations. At times those voices or your own inner voice may not seem that different from the voice of the Holy Spirit. Here are several guidelines that may help you recognize His voice.

1 The Holy Spirit will never contradict what the Bible teaches. I once met a young Christian who explained a decision he made like this: "God had to take me outside of His will to bring me to the center of His will." In my mind, this man was trying to justify actions that were not in accordance with the Word of God. The Psalmist describes the Bible as a "lamp to my feet, and a light to my path" (Ps. 119:105). If your direction is not in line with the Bible, change your direction. Following the direction of Scripture is never wrong.

2 You will maintain your closeness to the Lord and your openness to His Holy Spirit through prayer. You cannot stay full of the Holy Spirit without spending time with Him in prayer. Jesus set the example for us. Luke 6:12 tells us that Jesus chose His twelve disciples after spending the night in prayer. Jesus' personal victory over the cross was won when He travailed in prayer in the Garden of Gethsemane.

61

3 If the Holy Spirit speaks to you, that impression or feeling will not go away. It may happen during times of prayer or in response to a sermon. As a result, you may feel impressed to respond or make a change in your life. The intensity of that feeling may increase or decrease over time and circumstances, but it will not disappear completely, especially during your prayer times with the Lord. Your human emotional response to a stirring presentation will dissipate over time. That is normal for everyone. However, the Holy Spirit works on eternal principles and values, and His word to you will stand the test of days, weeks, and even years.

4 The Holy Spirit will usually confirm what He speaks into your heart through others. That confirmation can come from those who are close to you or through those placed in authority over you: your pastor or other leaders. My first step after feeling that the Holy Spirit was asking me to become a missionary was to talk to Terry. We had been pastors for four years, and I was not sure of her response to this sudden change in our lives. She reminded me, "Isaac, God first called me to be a missionary when I was twelve." Actually, my call was a confirmation of hers.

Not everyone will affirm what God is doing in your life. Some will not see and will never agree with the way you feel God is leading you. But God will be faithful to continue speaking into your heart and to bring others across your path to confirm what He wants you to do.

At the same time, if the key Christians in your life cannot confirm what you are sensing, you might want to reevaluate what you are feeling. Everyone needs reality checks now and then, and God will place them along your path to guide you in the direction He wants you to go.

5 The Holy Spirit will use circumstances to confirm what He is telling you. If you believe the Holy Spirit is speaking to you about a particular direction in your life, He will bring people, situations, opportunities, and even miracles along your way to indicate that you are on the right path. You will encounter opposition along the way. But opposition alone does not mean you have misheard the voice of the Holy Spirit.

"Well, Isaac, when are we going to start those last three church-es?" My friend Harry, a Christian businessman, looked at me across the thermal pool, but his words made me shiver. I was with Harry and his construc-tion team in the northern part of Uruguay. We had taken a break from our work one afternoon to enjoy the heated thermal pools near the church we were helping.

> The Holy Spirit will give you the abilities and will provide the resources to fulfill His will.

Terry and I had returned to Uruguay a year earlier, ready to add the last three churches to the seven God had helped us to found dur-ing our previous term. But things had not gone as we had planned. The drug rehabilitation center we had been assisting was in a deep financial crisis. We prayed, talked, then prayed some more before using the funds that we had reserved for those last three churches to help the young men and women walking through the process of deliverance from drugs through the power of Jesus Christ. We even raised more funds for the center. We had no regrets, just quiet resignation to the fact that our funds were depleted.

Harry didn't know what had happened. He just knew of our vi-sion to plant ten churches. Harry's words were God's confirmation to me, and they were soon followed by His provision. Within just a few months, God provided thousands of dollars, five construc-tion teams, three amazing pastoral families, and the support of the Uruguayan national church. Today, ten churches are scattered around the outskirts of Montevideo. Some are larger, some are smaller, but all are reaching their communities with the good news of Jesus Christ.

It doesn't matter if God has asked you to leave your home cul-ture to plant a church or drive a group of fourth graders to sum-mer camp. If He has called you, He will provide!

6 The Holy Spirit will give you the abilities and will provide the resources to fulfill His will. I knew little about church plant-ing and less about church construction when we began with the first four churches. One of God's first gifts to me was a young man named Santiago. He became my construction foreman for all ten of our church plants and many other projects all over Uruguay. He didn't tell me until much later that he had very little experience in running a construction crew when we started. But he grew into an experienced partner whom I could trust with anything—from handling thousands of dollars in donated construction funds to efficiently organizing the work at multiple construction sites. Like a key fitting into a lock to open a door, God will lead you into places where you and your abilities will fit to solve a problem or meet a need. God wants you to succeed.

Full of faith. Being full of faith is like climbing a tall tree and going out on a limb only to turn around and cut the limb between you and the tree! You know that you will fall if God does not supernaturally hold that limb in place, but you continue sawing because you have faith that He will.

Jesus told us that if we have a faith the size of a tiny mustard seed, we can move mountains. The writer of Hebrews gives us example after example of what faith looks like in chapter 11 of his book. By faith, Abraham offered his son as a sacrifice. By faith, a prostitute saved her family's life by cooperating with the Jewish spies.

Barnabas took many steps of faith, from selling his property and giving the funds to the apostles, to working with young Saul, to moving to Antioch. Each decision was a statement of faith that God was going to lead him and bless his actions.

Alejandro was a young leader in a local church in Montevideo as well as a skilled builder. He and his wife, Alicia, were comfortable with two incomes and their own home. When I sat down with the young couple at their home church to talk about their taking a huge step of faith—planting a new church—Alejandro was cautious. They would be starting from zero: no people, no building, and no experience pioneering a new outreach. I could sense that something happened as we were talking, but I could also see the uncertainty in the young man's eyes. He asked me for a week to consider our proposal. The feeling of sawing off that secure limb connecting them to their

> To become full of faith, you must begin by taking steps of faith now.

church and jobs was very strong. Yet when I called them the next week, they said yes.

Beginning the new work was very difficult for the young couple. They lacked workers to help with their children's outreach that drew the neighborhood kids every Saturday. Then, soon after construction of the new church began, hurricane-force winds blew down the wooden framework of the building and destroyed the campaign tent. It was an exhausting time for them, but Alejandro and Alicia continued to believe that God would raise up a strong group of believers in their community. They replaced the tent and built a new structure. When I visited the church on their third anniversary, a packed-out building greeted me. A full worship team, two children's choirs, a women's choir, and a drama team all had a part in the service. I was amazed to see the results of a young couple who was full of faith.

To become full of faith, you must begin by taking steps of faith now. God will often lead you along unclear paths where you can see only a step or two ahead. You won't know exactly where it will lead—up a hill or through a shadowy valley—but taking the first few steps is crucial.

The writer of Hebrews calls faith the "substance of things not seen" (Heb. 11:6). How can it be substantial if you can't see it? Its "substance" comes from dependence and confidence in God, who is guiding you. God is substantial. He is the personal God who created the universe.

The Scripture describes Barnabas as full of the Holy Spirit and faith. He depended on the leading of the Holy Spirit throughout his ministry and saw great miracles. Imagine the faith Barnabas placed in the Holy Spirit in journeying to Tarsus to look for young Saul. Imagine the faith Barnabas placed in Saul in bringing him back to Antioch to minister at his side. I think some of the greatest miracles in Barnabas' ministry were Paul's and Mark's later work. Imagine what God will do through you as you learn to listen to the voice of the Holy Spirit and take amazing steps of faith!

Work

*So Barnabas went to Tarsus to look for Saul,
and... he brought him to Antioch*

Barnabas pulled a smoking branch from the fire to stir the dying embers. The trip back to Antioch was long, almost seven days, and they were spending the night along the shores of the Mediterranean Sea. Taking a ship from Tarsus would have been much quicker than skirting the sea by land. But walking gave them time—time to talk and time to listen, although conversation had been scarce since they had left the city.

Finding Saul in Tarsus had been no problem. Barnabas had just asked for the Jewish tent makers with the rambunctious son. Barnabas had explained how God was adding many converts to the new church in Antioch. Some were Jewish, but there were Gentiles as well, desperate for solid teaching from the Word. Barnabas needed help discipling the growing congregation. And Saul had agreed to come.

Now Saul sat and stared into the fire. Barnabas felt more than saw the young man's gaze shift to study Barnabas' face in the warm reflection of the firelight. "So why did you come back for me?" Saul ventured, adding with a hint of bitterness, "No one else has even checked on me."

Memories of years before in Jerusalem flashed through Barnabas' mind. Saul's first attempt at ministry resulted in disputes and finally death threats. Saul attacked the preaching of the gospel with the same zeal he had earlier used to attack the church, and the results were almost the same. For both his and the church's safety, Saul had needed to leave.

Satisfied with the renewed flames, Barnabas dropped the stick back in the fire. It would accomplish nothing to tell Saul about the peace that had descended on the church after he left the area or about the numbers of new believers that had been added in his absence. Instead, Barnabas leaned toward Saul and looked him in the eye. Reflecting the sentiment that flooded his heart, he replied in a strong voice, "I believe God has something special planned for your life, Saul. He hasn't given up on you, and I want you to know that neither have I."

(Based on Acts 11:25)

Barnabas' trip to Tarsus demonstrated his desire to do what others were not willing to do. It seemed almost second nature to him and set him apart from many leaders in the early church. He befriended Saul at a time when the apostles were not willing to take that chance. Later, he would give Mark another opportunity when even Paul was unwilling to do so.

Jesus did not only what no one else *could* do but also what no one else *would* do. During the three years of His earthly ministry, Jesus constantly confounded the Jewish leadership and left the crowds who followed Him in wonder. He touched a leper that no one else would touch. He spared the life of a woman caught in adultery that the crowd wanted to stone.

"Today I will do what others won't, so tomorrow I can accomplish what others can't." Those words come from Jerry Rice, named in 2010 as the greatest player in NFL history. Rice set many records as a wide receiver but is perhaps best known for his work ethic. He showed up at practices early, attended rookie camps, and sat in special team meetings just to set an example. His teammates remember him for his daily run up "The Hill" in Edgewood County Park, California. It's a steep, two-and-a-half-mile climb to the top, and Rice would sprint up the hill every day to improve his physical conditioning.[8] His constant hard work and dedication led to his tremendous achievements.

> "Today I will do what others won't, so tomorrow I can accomplish what others can't."
> Jerry Rice

In his book *Outliers: The Story of Success*, Malcolm Gladwell tracks many top achievers in history, from Microsoft's Bill Gates to the Beatles to Mozart, looking for common indicators for their success. When asked about the cause of their success, many of these leaders attributed it to luck or being in the right place at the right time. But Gladwell dug below the surface and discovered that, in most cases, a crucial factor in the rise of these achievers was what he called "the 10,000-hour rule." In other words, the difference between those who become very good in their chosen area and those who are truly great is the dedication to invest ten thousand hours of practice or work. "The people at the very top don't work just harder, or even harder than everyone else. They work much, *much* harder."[9] Very simply, those who achieve great accomplishments do what others will not do.

Hard work is more than just the amount of effort exerted or sweat expended. It is an attitude that affects the way you do everything. It has two parts: focused determination and unrelenting perseverance.

Focused determination. Determination is the firm intention to achieve a desired end. Leaders who distinguish themselves come to a point of unwavering determination to accomplish their goals. When it came to Saul, Barnabas was very determined. Any trip during the first century was fraught with danger. Tarsus was just shy of eighty miles from Antioch as the crow flies, much more through the countryside. Roads were not secure, and bandits were common. Barnabas' trip to and from Tarsus was a test of how badly he wanted to reunite with young Saul.

Frank King, chief executive of the XV Olympic Winter Games in Calgary, Canada, honored the participants of the 1988 games during the closing ceremonies with these words: "You have captured our hearts. And some of you have soared like eagles." The crowds immediately began crying, "Eddie! Eddie! Eddie!" Yet Michael "Eddie the Eagle" Edwards had won no medals as a ski jumper. In fact, he came in dead last in the seventy-meter and the ninety-meter ski-jump competitions.

Eddie had no corporate sponsors. He funded his training from his own pocket. He used borrowed equipment, wearing up to six pairs of socks to fit into his oversized ski boots. He was heavier than his competitors, and he constantly struggled to keep his thick glasses from fogging up under his ski goggles.[10] Yet Eddie's passion for the sport and determination to do whatever was required made him an Olympic athlete and won the respect of the crowds in Calgary and those who watched him around the world.

Luke describes the time when Jesus resolutely set His face toward Jerusalem and the time of His passion (Luke 9:51). His decision to go to the cross to give His life for humanity was foretold in Isaiah: "I have set my face like flint" (Isa 50:7).

Determination finishes what passion begins.

It was this determination that carried Jesus through the suffering, humiliation, and pain of the cross. And it was this determination that bought our salvation.

Determination carries leaders through the troubled and tough times that come to all. Barnabas' determination led him to go to Tarsus to find Saul. Young Saul's determination carried him through the years of isolation in Tarsus, and we see that flint-like determination throughout his writing.

Determination finishes what passion begins. The emotion and energy you experience at the beginning of a great project is not enough to carry you through to its conclusion. The initial emotion will evaporate like the morning mist on a summer day.

During our first four simultaneous church plants, Terry's and my workday usually began at 6:00 a.m. with construction and didn't end till after 10:00 p.m. or midnight when the last of the campaign services ended. This went on for the better part of a year. Despite the exhaustion, complications, and challenges, we were determined not to let the four new church-plant pastors and their young families down. Each had made a similar decision, leaving careers, churches, friends, and their own families to follow God's call to plant a church in a new community.

Unrelenting perseverance. Some see *perseverance* as just a synonym for *determination*. However, I have observed that many begin with determination to accomplish their goal but never finish their task. Dr. Jim Taylor calls perseverance "The Grind," or the repetitive and stressful, tiring and tedious work that must be plowed through to accomplish a goal or task.[11] Perseverance carries determination to the end. Because I am determined, I will persevere—usually in the face of hardship or opposition.

Barnabas persevered in his faith in Saul. The apostle never gave up on the man who would go on and become the most prolific writer in the New Testament.

Our current ministry involves translating a lot of books and articles into many languages. It is some of the most tedious work I have observed. Bishal moved from Nepal to Bangkok, Thailand, to translate the notes and articles for a Study Bible in Nepali. He worked all day long seated at a computer at the office, then took additional work back to his apartment after work hours. After a simple dinner, he continued his task till the late hours of the night. Bishal continued grinding through page after page, day after day. While translation of the study notes usually takes about three years, Bishal finished in a little over fifteen months.

Athletes go through the same grind, persevering through repetitions of weight training or running. The athlete's goal may be winning a race or lifting a certain amount of weight, but the focus of the day becomes one foot before the other or another repetition with the barbell. It isn't fun, but it must be done.

To beat The Grind, [Dr. Taylor] recommends striking a balance somewhere in the middle of the love-hate continuum. Managing to truly love The Grind—the paper pushing, the boring meetings, the bleary-eyed mornings when you punch the clock at your 9-to-5 job after pulling an all-nighter on your side project—rarely ever happens. On the other hand, openly hating The Grind is a recipe for burnout. That's why Dr. Taylor writes: "I suggest that you neither love nor hate The Grind; you simply accept it as part of the deal in striving toward success."[12]

Those who excel in prayer often face the same grind of spending time before the Lord. Master communicators spend hours studying and listening to other communicators, learning the skills that put them in demand at conferences. Skilled leaders persevere in the hard tasks that result in success, whatever those may be. They do what others will not do.

I proudly carry a scar on my right hand just below where my fourth finger is attached to my palm. It reminds me of one of my greatest challenges in army basic training: the monkey bars. The monkey bars were a metal ladder about eighteen feet long with friction-polished rungs that hung just high enough so that I couldn't touch the ground with my feet. I hated them. My lack of upper-body strength kept me from completing the hand-over-hand journey across and back again that was required to pass basic training. The grip of my hands always gave out, and I fell to the ground. It wasn't for lack of determination on my part. I tried and tried until the palms of my hands cracked and bled. My hands became so sore and bloody that I literally couldn't even grasp the bars. So I did pushups and squat thrusts—anything my hands would tolerate as I worked to strengthen my arms.

Then came that last physical training test. It was either conquer the monkey bars or repeat basic training. My hands had healed somewhat but were still painful. The memory of those two minutes still lives fresh in my mind: the jump up to the first bar, my surprise when I reached the end of the bars and twisted my body for the *first time* for the return. However, my memory of those next bars is not very clear. I remember only reaching the last bar, swinging down, and feeling an astonished joy.

What made the difference—the additional exercise, my healing palms, or perhaps supernaturally provided strength? Maybe all of that; I don't know. I do know that for long afterward I often "ran" the monkey bars, marveling at how easy the task had become because I hadn't given up.

What do determination and perseverance look like to you? To Barnabas these meant leaving the security of Antioch to look for

Saul. And they meant a continued belief that God wanted to use Saul in a special way.

As a leader, the hard work behind the scenes becomes a part of who you are, and it will define your leadership. Like Jerry Rice, do today what others won't do so that you can accomplish what others will only dream about.

Results

They met with the church and taught a great many people. And in Antioch the disciples were first called Christians

"Christian? That's what he called you?" Barnabas broke off *a piece of bread and passed the remainder to Niger, who was reclining to his left around the small table. It was rare for the five leaders to have a meal together. Usually, they were scattered across Antioch and busily doing the work of the Kingdom, meeting in homes, teaching about Jesus, and praying for the sick and needy. Barnabas looked at each man in turn—Niger, Lucius, Manaen, and, of course, Saul.*

Saul had changed in many ways since the years before in Jerusalem. His eyes still shone with fervor every time he spoke of his encounter with Jesus, but now there was a different tone in his voice. Instead of always being the first to speak, he often waited to hear what others would say. When Saul taught, he had more patience, especially with the Gentiles who knew nothing of the Jewish prophets or the Law. The young man often accompanied Barnabas when he went from house to house and when the groups came together on the first day of the week to celebrate the Lord's resurrection. Still, every so often Barnabas noticed that same look of fiery, fixed determination in Saul's eyes he had seen when Saul debated the Hellenists in Jerusalem.

Niger nodded and continued with his story. "I was walking through the city gate when one of the Roman soldiers caught my eye. He spat at me and laughed. 'You think you are something, you follower of the Nazarene? What did you call Him? The Christ, the anointed one? I was in Jerusalem when they killed Him. He's dead! You're nothing more than a little Christ, a Christian—that's it, a follower of the King of the Jews killed by His own people!'"

"What did you do?" Saul asked, his intense eyes seeming to bore right through his friend.

Niger answered, "I just looked up at him and said, 'He lives!' You would have thought I had drawn a sword! He drew his and took a step toward me. But then he stopped suddenly as though someone had tied a rope around him, and he could go no further. 'Be careful, Christian, or you might just join your living Christ!' he hissed and then turned away."

No one spoke for several moments. Finally, Saul broke the silence, saying quietly, "Little Christs. May we be so honored as to carry His name."

Barnabas' eyes widened. He observed his young protégé thoughtfully before taking another bite of bread.

(Based on Acts 11:26)

Everything we do has consequences. Hard work produces results, but those results may not be equal to the work expended. Jesus taught that in the parable of the sower in Matthew 13. The sower cast his seed in hard soil, thorny soil, and rocky soil with little return. However, the sower also planted in fertile soil. The miracle was in the multiplication of results—thirty, sixty, and even a hundred times what was sown.

Barnabas and Saul saw remarkable results from their hard work in Antioch. The church in Antioch, the first church established outside Jerusalem, was one of the jewels of the New Testament. Flourishing under Barnabas' leadership, it was truly an amazing church.

Antioch was an evangelistic church. The Bible states twice that many people were saved and added to this church (Acts 11:21, 24). One of the reasons Barnabas went to find Saul was to help with the growing number of new believers.

It was an influential church. Followers of Christ first earned the nickname "Christians" from their neighbors in Antioch. Although the title was intended as a sign of derision, it became a badge of honor that has endured for almost two thousand years.

It was a generous church. When a prophet named Agabus told the church about a famine that was coming to Jerusalem, they took a special offering to send to help the church there.

Antioch was a church that developed leaders. The list of prophets and teachers included Barnabas (the leader), Simeon, Lucius of Cyrene, Manaen, and Saul. Together, they led a church that was reported to number in the thousands.

It was a spiritual church. Worship and fasting were a part of their service to the Lord. No wonder God used that church to reach the world with the gospel of Jesus Christ!

Finally, **it was a sending church.** Barnabas and Saul were sent out on the first missionary journey from Antioch. As the recognized leader in the church, Barnabas had great influence on this growing group of believers. Barnabas was productive.

Leaders in the church that Jesus established are expected to generate results. In the parable of the talents found in Matthew 25:14–30, three servants were entrusted with varying amounts of money with just one requirement: each was expected to invest the funds and provide the master with an increase of his investment. The slothful servant was punished, not because he had lost what he had, but because he did not even try to produce the results expected by his master.

Two fundamental components of producing results are preparation and excellence.

> Leaders in the church that Jesus established are expected to generate results.

Preparation. You will never be able to handle more than what you are prepared to receive.

James, a missionary, was to be the guest speaker at the fortieth anniversary of a small but growing church in a city up-river from the capitol. The pastor eagerly shared that the church had been founded during the great tent revivals when a missionary evangelist had visited the country. The tent revivals drew over three thousand people in attendance. Many people were saved, and documented healings and miracles were common.

James had heard similar stories from many different corners of the country. The nation had enjoyed a move of God—true revival—during what was fondly remembered as the Golden Age for the national church. However, many of the large tent crusades with thousands in attendance had transitioned into small congregations with no more than thirty to forty members. Although many reasons were cited, the common theme was that leaders and pastors were not prepared to handle the thousands of converts who had filled the tents, and a large percentage of the harvest drifted away.

Yet there were a few notable exceptions. Pastors with strong administrative skills set up the leadership and structure their churches needed to disciple new Christians. The pastors who prepared for the harvest conserved it.

The Bible is full of examples of human preparation for heavenly blessing. In Genesis 41, Joseph interpreted Pharaoh's dream and made subsequent preparations for the coming famine. In 2 Kings 4, a widow gathered containers in preparation for the divine provision of olive oil at Elisha's command. The oil ran out when all the containers were full. At the Last Supper, in one of the most intense scenes in the New Testament between the disciples and their Master, Jesus instituted the sacrament of communion, washed the disciples' feet, foretold Peter's denial and Judas' betrayal, and left us with important kingdom principles. Yet, as Matthew, Mark, and Luke record, hours before all that the Savior instructed Peter and John to follow a man carrying a water jar to a house. They were to instruct the owner to make ready for Jesus and the other ten disciples. The high drama of the evening was thus carefully prepared for—the room was arranged, the Passover meal was purchased and prepared, the bowl in which Jesus would wash twelve pairs of feet was set out, the wine that would become the symbol of the new covenant in His blood was purchased, and so on.

A strong leader thinks ahead, prepares, anticipates what is coming. Do you want to reach the lost? How will you smoothly incorporate new Christians into the existing congregation? How will new believers develop healthy relationships within the church? Suppose you want to start a drug rehabilitation outreach. What will you do with those who come off the streets in response to the hope in Jesus that you offer them? What will you do if both men and women come to you? Where will you house them? How will you feed them?

Think about what the Lord is calling you to do. The depth of your faith in God to provide will be seen in the extent of your preparation.

Excellence. Terry and I spent the first year of our married life in Germany and a good part of our free time touring the country. Ancient castles and cathedrals dominated many of the city skylines as well as the countryside. One cathedral we visited displayed one of its steeples on the ground in the courtyard. Its twin still adorned the top of its tower far above us. Underneath the lower steeple's multi-faceted slate peak was an incredible display of small, intricate stone carvings set in several "windows," perhaps over one hundred in all. I looked up at the tower and then back down at the steeple. I asked why anyone would put so much work and detail into something that no one could appreciate from a hundred feet away on the ground. I will never forget the tour guide's answer: "It was made for God to see."

> Excellence is the lens through which effective leaders view everything they do.

Paul dropped the biblical principle of excellence into his teaching in 1 Corinthians 10:31: "Do all for the glory of God." This takes excellence from just doing or being the best to another level. What does the Creator of the universe think of your effort? As with the steeple, He is the ultimate and best observer of all you do.

Excellence is the lens through which effective leaders view everything they do. It is not enough to just get the job done; the task is complete when every aspect is finished as if God were going to walk by and make a personal inspection.

Excellence is the scale by which you measure all you do. Debbi Fields took a bet from her husband that she could sell fifty dollars' worth of cookies on her first day of business. She sat in her storefront waiting for customers to come in until she realized that she about to lose her wager. "So I took to the streets. I walked up and down the street, letting people try the product, and that day I ended up selling $75 worth."[13] Ultimately, Mrs. Fields turned her love of cookies into a 450-million-dollar company. Her company's philosophy is "Good enough never is."

Excellence is rarely accomplished by a few big steps, but rather by innumerable small ones. A few years ago, the United Nations honored a simple farmer from Burkina Faso for his efforts to stop the Sahara Desert's continuing southern encroachment on the African continent. Yacouba was simply trying to provide a way for his family to eat. He dug lots of small pits about the size of a large paint can in the sun-baked African ground, then filled them with manure or other organic matter. The pits trapped the scarce rainfall, allowing crops to grow on previously abandoned land.

Yacouba used a small hoe to dig one small pit at a time, hour after hour, day after day. Although others ridiculed him as a madman, Yacouba persisted with his small pits. Jealous neighbors once burned over ten acres of his crops and newly planted forest. But Yacouba continued, replanting and sharing his farming technique with those who would listen. Today, dying communities are growing again because of the persistence of one man digging one small pit at a time.[14]

How did Barnabas prepare for the growth of the church in Antioch? He developed a leadership team. He brought Saul back from Tarsus. How did Barnabas demonstrate excellence? Read again the list of everything the church at Antioch was involved in. Antioch set the biblical standard of what a healthy church should look like.

Prepare for what you feel God wants to do through you. Do it with excellence. He will surprise you with the results ... or perhaps He won't surprise you so much if you are ready!

Empowerment

Paul and his companions set sail from Paphos and came to Perga in Pamphylia. And John left them and returned to Jerusalem

Barnabas spread his feet slightly and grasped the rail as another ocean swell lifted the ship's bow. The reflection of the three-quarter moon sparkled over the water, and the sail snapped as it filled with a new gust of wind. The captain had told them that if the winds held, the ship would arrive in Perga sometime tomorrow afternoon. Cyprus had already disappeared into the distance behind them. Young John Mark hung his head over the side and promptly lost the rest of his supper.

Things had not gone as Barnabas had imagined. Cyprus was his home, but Saul had quickly distinguished himself in their conversations with the Jewish community. Then, since the Roman proconsul, Sergius Paulus, had summoned them, Barnabas thought their group would have little trouble at the meeting. However, he had been amazed and more than a little frightened when Saul squared his shoulders and rebuked Bar-Jesus, a Jewish magician who had somehow wormed his way in and mocked their presentation of the Christ. "You son of the devil, you enemy of all righteousness, full of deceit and villainy ..." Saul had called down blindness on the man, and the sorcerer went blind! Sergius had been shaken, as had everyone else except Saul—or rather Paul, as he wanted to be called now. The intense look in his eyes had reminded Barnabas of Peter when he rebuked Ananias and then Sapphira. It was obvious the Holy Spirit was using Paul in a new way. Sergius had believed in Christ, and as they finished their time in Cyprus, Paul had begun to speak and walk with an increased sense of confidence.

81

Mark wiped his mouth and turned to his cousin. "What are you going to do? I thought you were in charge of this trip." His face was a mottled gray. Mark had been sick for most of the previous voyage from Antioch to Cyprus too, and his attitude toward Barnabas and especially Paul had turned dark in recent days. Having known Christ personally, Mark struggled to accept the former persecutor of the church as a brother and now a leader.

"The Holy Spirit is in charge of this trip," Barnabas answered without taking his eyes off the horizon.

"You know what I mean! He is taking over more and more," Mark managed before once more leaning his head over the ship's rail.

Barnabas didn't reply. Images of the past years with Saul raced through his mind: their first meeting in Jerusalem, Saul's return to Tarsus, his own trip to find Saul, and their year of ministry together in Antioch. He had watched Saul grow into a trusted leader in the church. Then came that powerful prophecy: "Set apart for me Barnabas and Saul." And now all of this.

Finally, Barnabas turned and faced Mark. "You and I both can see how the Lord is working through Paul." The young man quickly looked up when his cousin used Saul's Greek name. Barnabas continued, "I have always known that God was going to use him in powerful ways to spread the truth about Christ. Who am I to try to stop what the Holy Spirit is doing? No, Mark, if the Lord has opened a new door in Paul's ministry, I want to help that happen in any way I can."

"No matter what?" Mark asked.

"As long as it's the Lord," Barnabas replied.

Mark shook his head before turning and stumbling back to the hold where his belongings were stored. Barnabas watched him go and wondered aloud, "How much longer will you be with us, Cousin?"

Not long at all, apparently. Soon after they docked, Mark caught the next ship for home.

(Based on Acts 13:4–13)

// "Let the Prince win his spurs." Aslan's words from *The Chronicles of Narnia: The Lion, Witch, and the Wardrobe* empowered young Peter to defeat the wolf that was attacking his sisters. The great lion, Aslan, though capable of destroying the ravaging beast with a stroke of his own claws, allowed Peter to face, fight, and defeat his attacker. In doing so, Peter fulfilled a knight's quest of honor that would make him worthy of his own set of golden spurs and began his journey toward becoming the High King over Narnia.[15]

Every future leader must learn how to step to the front of the battle line to face his or her own challenges in life. Strong leaders empower those who come under their influence to do this. Jesus sent seventy-two followers out to share the gospel of the Kingdom, two by two, with specific instructions designed to stretch their faith: "Carry no moneybag, no knapsack, no sandals, and greet no one on the road" (Luke 10:4). The challenge was to develop relationships with people who would accept the message and help them as they shared the good news of Jesus Christ. Jesus knew that His time with them was short and that the leaders of His church needed to be prepared for ministry without depending on His physical presence.

In Barnabas' case, Saul was suddenly thrust into the limelight of their ministry when God used him powerfully before the Roman proconsul. In a matter of a few short verses, "Barnabas and Saul" (Acts 13:2, 7) changed to "Paul and his companions" (v. 13). We don't know how Barnabas felt about transitioning from his position as the group leader to supporting Paul's new prominence. But we do know the outcome of their continued ministry together.

Empowerment begins in your heart as a leader. The level of your self-confidence can be measured by the amount of control and authority you are willing to delegate to those who work with you. The more uncertain you are of your position and power, the more difficult it will be to acknowledge others' achievements or to allow another to share some of your responsibilities.

> Strong leaders empower others to step to the front of the battle line.

A Google search of "employee empowerment" results in over seven million possible links, and "employee appreciation" brings up more than six million links. You can find seven steps, ten steps, twenty steps, suggested exercises, lists of empowering phrases leaders can use—everything you can imagine to help leaders empower those they supervise. Yet for all the available tools and helps, empowerment continues to be one of the greatest challenges that leaders at all levels face.

Knowledge about how to empower is not enough. Until you make empowerment part of who you are, information like the guidelines that follow will probably mean little more to you than another list. Do what it takes, and make the changes that will take you to another level of leadership—a level of empowerment that inspires others to strive to do the same. How do you make those changes? Start by asking God. He always answers!

So what does it look like to empower the people you lead?

Listen to your people's calls, dreams, and visions. Just as God is leading you as you follow your own call, He is working in the lives of those around you. And more than likely, their primary call is not just to enhance your ministry. Rather, the Lord has brought your paths together for a season so that each can complement the other to advance His kingdom.

Effective leaders take the time to learn about what each team member feels called to do, what he or she dreams about, or perhaps whether he or she has a vision for the future. Many times, especially in the lives of younger believers, such a dream or vision is not fully developed. It may well evolve or change over the course of time, perhaps because of your influence in the person's life. That vision, regardless of how realistic or far off it may seem, is precious to its owner and merits your highest respect.

"Carina, I was wrong!" I told the young woman standing before me. Carina had become an effective and dependable lay leader in the church I was visiting. I remembered the day, years before, when I had interviewed her as part of her application to enroll in Bible school. Carina struggled with severe dyslexia, so much so that it was difficult for her to read. I recommended that she study in her church instead of attempting the years of rigorous study, but she was adamant about enrolling. Over the next four years, I watched her work hard to overcome her limitations and grow into a leader among the student body. Carina's drive came from her dream of finishing Bible school. She graduated. Now she was a wife and mother and one of the "go-to" people at her church. I thank the Lord that Carina refused to allow me to derail her dream. She taught me a valuable lesson. One of my personal goals since that time has been to encourage and empower everyone the Lord brings across my path. He knows what He is doing much better than I do.

Plan for your people to succeed. They want to succeed, and your recognition and support of their efforts will have an unforgettable impact on their lives. Here are some practical steps you can use to make that a reality.

1 Clearly define what success looks like, then hang on to that definition. Most of us played the game Keep Away as children. The game involves a couple of usually bigger kids tossing a ball back and forth between themselves, trying to keep it away from the reach of one or more younger kids. It can be a lot of fun if the younger ones don't lose hope of grabbing the ball. As long as they believe they have a chance of success, they will run, jump, and at times devise original strategies to get that ball.

One of the quickest ways to foster discontent and defeat in life is to keep moving the target for success. Clearly defined goals may be difficult to create and attain. However, if the goals are consistent and achievable, you will see incredible results in the lives of those you oversee as they strive to meet those goals.

Terry and I saw the value of establishing clearly defined and achievable goals with our church planters in Uruguay. We could not guarantee our new pastors that the baby congregations they were planting would grow, but we could set goals for our pastors to reach. Each pastor and spouse researched and wrote a report about their community that included a short history, the names of influential people like police chiefs and mayors, and a map with all the worship centers identified. Each went door to door to personally meet everyone who lived near the new church site and conducted a series of prayer walks that covered the entire community. And it worked. Our pastors came to know and be known by the people around their churches. One pastor always took his baby as he went door to door. He laughed as he told me people who might not normally take the time to talk to him would gladly stop to see his little one. Each pastor built a history of small successes along the path of establishing a new church.

2 Celebrate successes and mourn losses. Achievements, birthdays, anniversaries, graduations, illnesses, and deaths—everything that is important to those who work with or for you should be recognized. Every day, Facebook notifies me about those who are celebrating birthdays. I go through the list, sending short "Happy Birthday" notes. One reason for the time I take with the notes is that I enjoy reading the same messages sent to me on my birthday. Do for others what you would have them do for you. That's biblical!

> Dealing with issues before they become intractable problems will help you and your people.

3 Give feedback, correct problems, and then move on. Feedback is vital for those who are stepping into new areas of work and ministry. You must also recognize and deal with the mistakes and problems that will come along. Many leaders are reluctant to face possible conflict, so they put off dealing with problems until they get angry enough. Dealing with issues before they become intractable problems will help you and your people.

Dealing with problems involves a journey that moves the participants toward dealing with the difficult realities and choices that will bring needed changes. It's important to accompany these hurting people as they move on and return to regular, healthy routines of life. Just as a cast is removed and thrown away after the broken bone it once protected is whole, corrected problems should be left in the past.

Empowerment defined Barnabas' work with Paul. From Tarsus to Antioch to Cyprus and further in the continuing story, Barnabas allowed Paul to grow in his ministry. Scripture shows us the beginnings of Barnabas' similar work with Mark. Has God brought someone into your life whom you can encourage and perhaps empower toward greater things than you have done?

Release

"You're not one to stay at an inn, are you, my friend?" Barnabas observed as Paul stretched the coarse layer of woven goat hair over the frame of branches he had cut and lashed together. The two men were one day out of Perga with another four days to go before reaching the major crossroads city of Antioch of Pisidia.

Paul laughed. "I wouldn't be much of a tent maker if I were! Besides, inns are dangerous places, and do you remember how long it took to get rid of the fleas we picked up the last time we overnighted at an inn?" Paul gauged the distance for the tent support rope and began hammering a stake into the ground with the rock he had carefully chosen as his tool. Earlier Paul had spent a good half hour examining and testing various candidates before selecting the right stone: round with one flat surface, not too heavy, but solid enough to keep from splitting when he drove the stakes in the ground.

Barnabas smiled as he stepped down to the stream that gurgled over the stones from which Paul had selected his hammer. He bent down and scooped up a quick drink. "Carefully chosen." The words rolled over in his mind as Barnabas walked along the streambed.

"Father, I have no idea what we should do once we arrive in Antioch," he prayed. Barnabas knew the leaders of the local synagogue would recognize him as a Levite and Paul as a Pharisee and would probably give them an opportunity to speak. He also remembered what had happened to Paul when he first began preaching Jesus in Jerusalem and now

89

just days ago in Cyprus. Conflict and turmoil seemed to follow his young companion every time he opened his mouth.

"Maybe I should do the preaching," Barnabas wondered aloud. He glanced at the water and saw a rock similar to the one Paul was pounding with up the hill. "Carefully chosen." The words came to his mind again, their meaning now as clear as the water that flowed around the rock. The apostle reached out and plucked the rock from the stream. He felt its weight and tossed it in the air, catching it with his other hand. "Thank You, Father!" Barnabas whispered, then headed back toward the sound of hammering.

"Paul," he called, stopping his friend in mid-swing, "what would you think of being the principal speaker in Antioch Pisidia?"

(Based on Acts 13:14–16)

Both Paul's and Mark's ministries continued far beyond the men's time with Barnabas, showing that one of Barnabas' greatest strengths was his ability to release them to minister. Barnabas' permission freed Paul to utilize his unique skills as a communicator.

What can you do to give permission and freedom to those you lead?

1 **Release your people to try.** One of the greatest challenges you will face as a leader is allowing those under you to excel in the areas of their giftings. They will not do things as you would. If you are gifted in the same areas, they may not do as well as you. However, with your permission to try, they may even surpass your own accomplishments. Releasing means having enough confidence both in yourself and in those who work with you to tell them, "Yes, you can!"

> Releasing means having enough confidence both in yourself and in those who work with you to tell them, "Yes, you can!"

The first step in releasing the gifts and abilities of the people who work with you is openness. Give them a chance. Henry began his first month as children's pastor full of ideas. He wanted to talk them over with the lead pastor, who had previously held Henry's position. Henry tapped on the office door and asked for a minute of the man's time. The pastor waved him in while finishing an e-mail. Henry began to ask about signing kids in for Sunday morning children's church when his pastor interrupted him with a quick "No!" and then laughed. Henry halfheartedly chuckled with him, but tried again, noticing that the pastor's attention kept flicking back to the monitor as e-mails popped up on his server. As the young man finished, the pastor almost imperceptibly shook his head, then explained to Henry that he needed to wait a few more weeks to learn the culture of the church before suggesting changes. He asked Henry if he had anything else. Thinking the right answer was probably "No," Henry responded in kind before heading back out the door.

Release can occur overtly, such as through conversations, meetings, or e-mail. However, the most impactful releases are much subtler. Roughly 90 percent of communication is nonverbal. Cues from your facial expressions, your tone, and your actions will reveal your true thoughts about what those who answer to you are saying.

This is a skill I am still learning. Over the past few years, I have begun the practice of actively focusing on anyone who steps into my office. I turn away from what I am doing, roll my chair to the corner of my desk, and look my guest in the eyes. Then I strive to allow the individual to finish his or her thought before I speak. This gives my guest value and the release to talk openly, which can lead to the all-important first steps of trying something new—something the person may not have attempted without feeling that release. And if I happen to disagree with the person's proposal, I can express it in an affirming way that gives him or her permission to try again.

One misconception that haunts many leaders is the belief that the success of those they lead will diminish their own worth. Part of King Saul's curse was his fear that the young man playing the harp across the room would replace him one day as king of Israel. Twice he tried to take young David's life. The third time David escaped and spent years on the run.

Some see success like a pie with a limited number of slices. If you take a slice, that's one less for me. And if your slice is bigger than mine, I am diminished. However, I have come to believe that achievement and success multiply and grow like yeast in bread. Given the right conditions, successes will spread from one lump of dough to another, causing all to rise.

2 Allow your people to struggle their way to success. It was 4:30 a.m. and we hadn't closed our eyes all night. Our boot-camp drill instructors had kept us up all night cleaning the grouting in the tile floor with toothbrushes. Now they stomped in, yelling for everyone to assemble outside our barracks for transportation to the physical training (PT) field for a test.

We groaned as the trucks off-loaded our company of trainees. I decided that I and everyone else in the company had had enough and marched up to one of our leaders. "Drill Sergeant," I huffed, "this is completely uncalled for! None of us have slept, and now you expect us to take this PT test! I am going to talk to the company commander as soon as I can!"

The drill sergeant just looked at me from under his flat-brimmed, felt hat, smiled, and said, "Ok, Smythia," then walked away.

We took the test and were amazed to learn that we achieved our highest scores to date for a PT test. We all learned that we were more capable than we had ever dreamed. It took staying up all night before taking the test to find that out. But the drill sergeant knew I never would have learned that life-changing lesson without facing the struggle. I never did speak to the company commander.

Most experienced leaders have already faced many of the challenges that those under them are working through. You will be tempted to rescue those who struggle, but that will not help them to grow and develop their own solutions to challenges. Listen and encourage them when they come to you with their problems. Explore possibilities, but keep the responsibility for solutions squarely on the shoulders of those who ask for your help and guidance. This can be hard to do when you quickly see solutions they cannot yet see.

Driving up the hill between the Uruguayan Bible school and the airport was never a concern to me, but it was a tremendous challenge for Jason, our sixteen-year-old, who was learning to drive our stick-shift van. We had practiced in the safety of a large park with driving trails, but this was his first time to drive on the roads. The van bucked and stalled in the middle of the road when Jason shifted into the wrong gear to climb the hill. My heart began to pound as he struggled to start the vehicle and engage the clutch. I'm sure it was only a few seconds, but it seemed like an eternity of starting and stalling. Finally, Jason gunned the accelerator and dropped the clutch, spinning the wheels and heading up the hill. It was a difficult lesson for my teenage son but much more so for me. My inclination was to pull my son out of the driver's seat and danger, but I held off just long enough for my son to succeed.

> Rescuing those who struggle will not help them to grow and develop their own solutions to challenges.

Jesus directly answered only three of 183 questions posed to Him in the New Testament. Many of His responses came in the form of another question. His goal was much more than to simply provide answers. Rather, it was to produce growth and change in others' lives.

3 **Allow your people to grow in their relationship with you.**
I first met seventeen-year-old identical twins Ben and Samuel when they moved to our Bible school with their parents, who had accepted the position of on-campus student supervisors. For the next several years, I walked alongside these two young men as they grew into young leaders. They both enrolled as students, and we dealt with the unique challenges for these young men for whom the Bible school campus was home. They became my students, and I occasionally wondered as I listened to their first attempts at sermons, graded their papers, and worked through their minor discipline bumps just how they would be as pastors. They also worked for me on the construction of several buildings during summer breaks.

Both are now married with families and pastoring growing churches. I once showed up unexpected at a youth service where

Sam was preaching. He told the story of when I had assigned him and Ben the job of running underground piping about thirty feet away from the downspouts of the classrooms to a huge ornamental rock we had placed in the middle of the campus's large courtyard.

Sam told us how he and his brother thought it was too much work to run the pipes to the rock. They decided it would be far easier to move the rock closer to the buildings. They vainly struggled for two hours to move the rock until they realized they could have finished the task long before if they had simply dug the shallow ditch for the pipes. I had never known of their attempted modification of my orders. We all laughed until our sides hurt as Sam described their useless sweat, struggle, and strain.

> Do you trust the Lord enough to let others do things that you might do better?

After that service, I began to reevaluate my relationship with these young men. It was time to move past "Brother Isaac and the Garcia boys." I decided to begin calling them Pastor Samuel and Pastor Ben and to treat them as proven pastors.

Jesus often chided His disciples for not grasping what He was trying to teach them. They were in a three-year training program that stretched and shaped them into the apostles who carried the gospel to the world. But after His resurrection, Jesus' relationship with His followers changed. I believe one of reasons Christ ascended was to draw a clear line in His relationship with His followers. He could have just stopped appearing to them, but He made His departure one of the foundational stones in the church's history with some of the most important teachings. Days later, the Holy Spirit took Jesus' place as the apostles' Counselor.

Somewhere between Cyprus and Antioch in Pisidia, Barnabas made the decision to release Paul to exercise his giftings. It certainly didn't always go well. But Barnabas had faith in his position in Christ and in Paul's calling. What's your confidence level? Do you trust the Lord enough to release those around you to try and perhaps even fail? Do you trust the Lord enough to let others do things that you might do better? That's leadership the Barnabas way.

Success

"Well, that was unexpected." Paul limped into the outer room *and spoke as calmly as if he had found an extra bit of meat in his soup bowl. Barnabas rolled his eyes. He and Paul had lived on the ragged edge of crisis and miracles for the past weeks. Beginning in Cyprus, a pattern had emerged: The two apostles preached Jesus Christ in the local synagogues, and the Jews rejected their message and stirred up opposition. But the Gentiles opened their doors and hearts to the gospel, and God responded with miracles.*

Then there was Lystra. Lystra was a disaster sandwiched between two miracles. God had healed a well-known citizen who had never walked before in his life. The people were amazed! There was no denying what the Lord had done. Yet instead of bringing glory to God and attention to Jesus Christ, the miracle prompted the residents to call Barnabas "Zeus" and Paul "Hermes," both local idols. Paul had wanted to use the moment to preach to the raucous crowd, but Barnabas thought it better to retire for a while until things calmed down. Then came word from the local temple that the heathen priests had organized a sacrifice of oxen to be made to Paul and Barnabas.

Barnabas had called to the back room for Paul and run out the door, Paul at his heels. The mob at the temple was loud, boisterous, and almost uncontrollable. Some were there because of the miracle. Others had no idea what was going on. They didn't even notice Barnabas until he climbed halfway up a statue of Zeus and shouted at the top of his lungs. Paul joined him, both of them ripping their garments at the neck.

Finally, the noise had abated enough for the apostles to plead for the lives of the two hapless animals already bound on the bronze altar. The mood had darkened as the priests and then others realized the two speakers wanted nothing to do with their gods. In fact, they represented another God, one who threatened the people's livelihood. By the time the apostles had finished, the crowd was much reduced and sullen. The miraculous healing had been forgotten.

A few days afterward, Jewish leaders had arrived from Antioch and Iconium, determined to do everything in their power to stop Barnabas and Paul. The monotheistic Jews and the polytheistic Gentiles formed an unlikely alliance and began searching for the pair who were turning their worlds upside down. They found Paul and stoned him, dragging his body out of the city past the temple where they had earlier tried to worship him. They summarily tossed him out like rotting garbage.

Soon after the crowd had disbursed, Barnabas and a small group of new believers had gathered in shock around Paul's broken body. Stoning was an ugly way to die. Then Barnabas watched in open-mouthed silence as the bloody body coughed and its chest rose. Someone on the far side of the group shouted when Paul slowly got to his feet. They began to sing loud praises to God, but Barnabas quickly quieted everyone in fear that the mob would return. They drew Paul into the center of their group and helped him go back into the city. That had all happened last night.

"Are you sure you are ready to travel, Brother Paul?" Barnabas asked incredulously.

Paul's body looked bruised and battered. He stretched slowly and replied, "I think so." Paul paused briefly, and his eyes took on that familiar intense look. "Who knows what they will do when word gets out that I'm not dead?" He adjusted one of the several bandages that wrapped his cuts. "Besides, the city of Derbe has yet to hear of Jesus."

Barnabas began to roll his eyes again but then stopped himself. At the very least, God had healed Paul, and at the most,

Barnabas may well have witnessed Paul's resurrection. Barnabas looked upward, and in his heart he prayed, "Lord, I thank You for the new Christians You have added to Your church. I thank You for the miracles. But Father, what next?"

Then Barnabas felt again the deep assurance in his spirit that he knew was from the Lord. He shrugged his shoulders and nodded his head. "Come on then, Paul." Barnabas stretched his arm toward his fellow traveler. "Lean on me until you work out the stiffness in your legs."

(Based on Act 14:8–24)

Bill's church had experienced the growth many pastors only dream about. Church attendance had doubled and now almost tripled, and Bill had added new staff. As he looked at their faces at planning meetings, gazing expectantly at him across the U-shaped formation of tables, Bill wondered what he had to offer them. So often Bill felt like he was making up answers and drawing up plans spontaneously without taking time to think and pray over decisions as he had done in the past. Yet something miraculous was happening.

There were many challenges. One of the greatest was his church board. The five members continued to view the church as though it were operating in the same way as two years before. They were hesitant to bring in additional staff and held unending discussions about the finances. How much should be held back for emergencies? What was a proper salary for the pastor of a growing church? End-of-the-year salary talks had been tense, leaving Bill questioning if they even understood the vision he had been casting.

> While failure may mean going back to familiar ground, success opens new and unknown pathways that require different responses to unfamiliar challenges.

The church's success meant demands on Bill's time were increasing, and he was forced to delegate most of the home and hospital visits he had previously loved. Sermon preparation time had to be carved out between endless meetings, paperwork, and phone calls or late at night when he needed to rest.

As he drove home after another long day of putting out little fires while trying to ignite big ones, his cell phone rang. He let it continue to ring as he debated whether he had the energy for another call. Bill finally shot a glance at his phone. It was an old ministry friend. Bill smiled and picked it up. Before he could say anything, he heard the familiar voice ask him, "Has anyone told you what a great job you are doing today?" Bill sighed a little and then laughed. "You're the first! You know, I almost didn't pick up the phone, but I'm glad that I did. The truth is, it's a little hard to feel much of anything besides tired right now," Bill admitted to his friend. Fifteen minutes later, Bill climbed from his car just as tired but not quite as burdened as when he climbed in.

Spiritual success is often defined as faithfulness to the call God has placed on your life. It is the subject of countless teachings and sermons. However, success that comes because of growth in a church or a ministry is another matter. For many leaders, that kind of accomplishment can be much harder to handle than failure. While failure may mean going back to familiar ground, success opens new and unknown pathways that require different responses to unfamiliar challenges.

Barnabas and Paul were accustomed to opposition from the Jews, but being taken for gods after the lame man was healed was a completely new challenge. Suddenly, Paul and Barnabas were lauded. Neither had experienced that before. It was all they could do to keep the crowd from idolizing them. Yet, in the end, Lystra almost ended their missionary venture. But for God's divine intervention after Paul was stoned and left for dead, we would not have his Epistles.

Those who learn how to adapt to the changes and avoid the pitfalls that success brings will turn that success into spiritual growth, both in their ministry and in their personal lives. Those who don't may follow a pattern we have seen before. For example, King David is honored as a man after God's own heart, a forerunner of Jesus Christ, yet he is also an example of how even a great leader can mishandle his own success.

Position. David was just a shepherd boy when Samuel anointed him to lead the nation of Israel. Barnabas and Paul were church leaders in Antioch when the Holy Spirit called them to take the gospel to the Gentiles. Those who find themselves in positions of authority, responsibility, and influence—no matter how they got there—face similar intended and unintended consequences of being in leadership.

> The prohibited line is not crossed in one giant step, but through a series of small ones.

Pressure. When your leadership skills take you to places you have never been, you will experience demands you have never faced. Young David's success brought the admiration of a nation and the jealously of a king. He was forced to flee for his life, live as a refugee, and serve a foreign king. However, with the death of King Saul, everything changed. David was recognized as king and began the process of consolidating his rule. This brought battles to extend his rule and influence as well as intrigue among his leaders. It was exhausting work. Leadership challenges can drain energy reserves as you work to build on the successes you have experienced.

Permission. Leaders use many coping strategies to handle the pressures they face. A common one is "giving yourself permission" to enjoy things you might not normally do. Upgrading to business class on a return flight, taking an extended vacation, asking a subordinate to pick up dry cleaning for you—doing things like these may help you stay focused on your important obligations. However, they are different from your norm and at some level require the decision to give yourself permission.

David gave himself permission to stay in Jerusalem while his generals and the army marched off to battle. The author of 2 Samuel notes that decision with a simple description: "In the spring of the year, the time when kings go out to battle, David sent Joab, and his servants with him, and all Israel. And they ravaged the Ammonites and besieged Rabbah. But David remained at Jerusalem" (11:1).

There was nothing necessarily wrong with David's decision to stay home while the army was out. But permission can become a first step to a problem.

Privilege. Feeling entitled to a privilege can carry you beyond the permissible into the prohibited. The reasoning is often similar to permission: "Since I am under this pressure, dealing with this stress, accomplishing this goal, I deserve this privilege." This is usually an unspoken, and sometimes unconscious, internal conversation.

Many times, the line is crossed not in one giant step but through a series of small ones. David decided to go out on his terrace. He noticed a beautiful young woman bathing on the next roof. He decided to continue to look. David asked his people about her and then sent word for her to visit him. Each small step drew him closer to a line he knew he shouldn't cross into adultery, deception, and finally murder.

Pastor Jose was the treasurer for a group of area pastors and responsible for a few thousand dollars of the group's money. One month, Jose came up short in his personal finances and borrowed a few dollars from the fund that he quickly paid back. A few months later, he found himself in a similar situation and borrowed a little more. However, this time he was not able to pay the money back for several weeks. This pattern continued until Jose had taken and misused most of the other pastors' funds. The pastors were shocked when the loss was discovered because all of them considered Pastor Jose to be a good pastor and a good friend.

One chorus of Handel's *Messiah* proclaims a powerful truth from Isaiah 53:6: "All we like sheep have gone astray." If you have listened to or sung this chorus, you will remember that the word *astray* is drawn out and sung high and low. The biblical truth is that regardless of your position or importance, you are a sheep, and sheep tend to go astray. Going astray will lead you down a convoluted path. But God does not intend for the pressures we assume to affect or destroy us or our leadership. The Isaiah passage concludes with the promise that God has laid the iniquity of us all on Him, Jesus Christ. There is a way out.

Accountability. The gripping story of David's sin and restoration continues in 2 Samuel 12. Later Jewish kings imprisoned and even killed those who delivered messages they did not want to hear. But King David allowed the prophet Nathan to hold him accountable. One of the most important decisions you can make as a leader is to allow someone who knows you well to speak into your life for good or bad. This is someone who has earned your trust and respect enough to tell you the truth without fear of retribution.

> One of the most important decisions you can make as a leader is to allow someone who knows you well to speak into your life for good or bad.

Your spouse should be the first person who can tell you things you don't want to hear. However, your husband or wife often experiences the same pressures and temptations you do and may not be as objective as a trusted friend or mentor outside your family circle.

Over the years, I have invited a few trusted friends to speak into my life without fear of losing my friendship. I have been honored to fill the same role in the lives of other friends. It's a hard decision—one that leaves you vulnerable to those who know both your good and not-so-good sides—but it will strengthen your leadership as the years go by.

Thorns. Paul was given "a thorn in the flesh" to keep him from being conceited from the revelations and ministry he experienced (2 Cor. 12:1–10). We don't know what it was, perhaps an eye problem or perhaps an adversary that he called "a messenger from Satan." But when Paul asked three times that the thorn be removed, the Lord's answer was, "My grace is sufficient for you, for my power is made perfect in weakness" (v. 9). God allows and leaves problems, struggles, and challenges in our path. They may be gifts designed to keep us dependent upon Him and His grace as the source of all that we accomplish.

Barnabas' and Paul's brush with success in Lystra brought disaster. Yet God intervened as He always does when invited. The two apostles leaned on each other as they continued their missionary journey. While we know little of how Barnabas handled the pressures of ministry, his partner needed a "thorn in the flesh" to keep him focused on God's grace.

How do you handle success and the pressures that accompany it? If you don't already have one, find a trusted Nathan to speak into your life. And if you are dealing with a thorn that won't go away no matter what you do, maybe you should stop fighting it and look for God's purpose behind it.

Generosity

They listened to Barnabas and Paul as they related what signs and wonders God had done through them among the Gentiles

Barnabas drew a deep breath and stood. The original apostles were seated to his left. From the corner of his eye, Barnabas caught Matthew's nod and encouraging smile. The din of conversation slowly died down as those who had gathered gave him their attention. People from both sides of the current controversy remembered Barnabas' ministry in Jerusalem and respected him. Yet the tension in the room hovered like smoke from a smoldering fire that threatened to leap back into flame at any moment.

The question of being circumcised and following the laws of Moses hung over all the believers in Jerusalem—the same city where Jesus had healed the lame on the Sabbath. Several converted Pharisees still wore their ceremonial robes with the distinctive blue borders on the bottom. For them there was no question. Observing the Law was part of serving the Messiah.

From their own experiences, Barnabas and Paul knew that the growing groups of new believers scattered across the Roman Empire needed to know what being a Christian meant. Did the Gentile believers have to convert to Judaism to become followers of Christ?

Peter stood in front of the assembly with his arm stretched toward Barnabas. "Barnabas and Paul have traveled throughout Cyprus and the regions of Mysia and Bithynia. Tell us, Barnabas, what have you found?"

A myriad of thoughts and feelings flooded Barnabas' heart in the few seconds it took to walk over into Peter's brotherly *embrace. His eyes scanned the crowd, recognizing several faces. These were his brothers and sisters in Christ, each with a personal story of faith and, for many, of suffering.*

His words came easily, recounting the early days and miracles at Antioch, then Cyprus, Perga and ... Barnabas stopped almost mid-sentence. He glanced at Paul, who was seated in the shadows beside a supporting column. Barnabas could make out the now-familiar gleam in Paul's eyes that told him his companion had something to say.

This was only the third time Paul had returned to Jerusalem and the first where he was with all the apostles and elders in one place since his humiliating departure for Tarsus. Barnabas turned toward him. "Brother Paul," he called out. Everyone's eyes followed his voice. "Come and share with the brothers and sisters more about Cyprus and of Lystra too."

(Based on Acts 15:1–21)

Great leaders are also generous leaders. Yet this kind of generosity is not measured by dollars and cents but by other increments: time, mercy, and honor.

Time. Sam and Bishop Cedric had known each other since before the latter's elevation to national prominence. Cedric had been Sam's pastor. Now they caught breakfast together every few months, in between the bishop's busy travel schedule and meetings. One morning, Sam arrived at his leader's office a few minutes early for a rescheduled meeting. After seeing another visitor to the door, Cedric walked with Sam back to his office. The two men talked for a few minutes before a call came for the bishop on his cell phone. He looked at his phone briefly, silenced it, and laid it facedown.

Seeing how busy Cedric was, Sam stood, saying he had taken enough of the bishop's valuable time. "Nonsense!" Cedric replied. "I have another thirty minutes before I have to take another meeting. Tell me about ..." Sam blinked involuntarily as the significance of those words sunk in.

Time is the one commodity that all share equally. However, as responsibility increases, time becomes more precious. Time spent on one project or appointment means time taken away from another. Many leaders learn principles of time management to help them maximize their use of what feels like a steadily shrinking resource.

Time invested demonstrates value imputed. You will spend more time with the people you value most. Jesus invested His three years of ministry into the lives of His disciples. Barnabas invested his time into Saul and later John Mark. Generosity with your time is a measurable marker of the value you place on those who work with and for you.

> Generosity with your time is a measurable marker of the value you place on those who work with and for you.

Yet investing time does not mean sacrificing important goals and deadlines on the altar of relationships. It does mean working hard to make the most of the moments you have. Imagine a pitcher of water. Being generous with your time means you pour out the last quarter of the pitcher with the same generosity of heart with which you poured out the first. The attitude you demonstrate toward any amount of time spent with those around you will say so much.

Mercy. "Blessed are the merciful, for they shall receive mercy" are Jesus' words as recorded in Matthew 5:7. Leaders are often placed in the unenviable positions of prosecutor, judge, and jury when they have to deal with problems. They must measure the needs of the offender against the standards of the organization they represent. The Jews of Jesus' day had weighted the standard of the Law until there was no room left for mercy. This provided the drama for the story of the woman caught in adultery. Her sin was apparent, and justice demanded she be stoned. Jesus' merciful response caught everyone by surprise and transformed the woman's life.

Barnabas was a generous mercy giver. That mercy led him to look for Saul, bring the young Pharisee back into fellowship and leadership, and eventually cede his position of authority to Paul. He did the same with Mark.

Stories of mercy givers capture our attention. National news outlets reported the story of a Maryland police officer who showed mercy on a young mother caught shoplifting diapers for her baby. Instead of arresting her, he paid for the diapers and gave them to her.[16]

However, how does mercy giving apply in the case of a young pastor caught in the act of purchasing pornography or of the church secretary found to be taking money from the church offerings? Here are some practical suggestions.

1 Generous mercy reacts sooner rather than later. Many times, the signs of problems are apparent long before action is taken. Weak leaders wait to do something until forced to by circumstances or by their own emotions. Just as good parents don't wait until their toddler is in the middle of the street to grab their little one, a good leader intervenes as soon as possible. Don't wait until you are angry to react. Base your motivation on the offender's need, not yours.

2 Generous mercy deals with the problem and saves the relationship. Many leaders view failures on the part of those they work with as personal betrayals. "How could you do this to me?" is a common reaction. However, most negative situations come from a constellation of underlying problems that may or may not have anything personal to do with the leader.

Pablo was a bright, soon-to-graduate Bible school student from a prosperous home in contrast to many of our poorer students. I liked Pablo and was so disappointed when I learned he had copied the work of another student. As academic dean, my job was to deal with the cheating that all the students knew about. Cheating was common in local high schools and colleges in this culture. What I did would not only affect Pablo but would also be an example to the student body. I made clear that Pablo would receive a zero for the class but that he had enough credits to still graduate. We talked about the importance of integrity as Christians, but I said nothing about my personal feeling of disappointment. Pablo went on, finished the semester, and graduated. Months later, he thanked me for what had become one of his greatest life lessons.

3 **Generous mercy aims for restoration and not punishment.**
The story of the Bible is the story of the restoration of humankind's
relationship with their Creator. Punishment is a terminal condi-
tion; it is a rope that lowers you into the pit and then withdraws.
But restoration leaves a ladder to climb back out. Restoration looks
toward the future. The theme verse for this book is Acts 11:25:
"Then Barnabas went to Tarsus to look for Saul." It does no harm
to the passage to add, "and he took a ladder with him." Make time
to resolve personal issues with those who work with you after a
difficult meeting. And keep that healing time in your mind during
the thorniest part of the meeting.

4 **Generous mercy has a short memory.** Knowledge of another's shortcomings can become a powerful weapon. I believe Stephen's dying words, "Lord, do not hold this sin against them,"
weighed heavily on Saul's mind until the time of his own encounter with Jesus Christ, and perhaps even after. I suspect those
words were the "goads" that Saul found so hard to kick against,
as Jesus mentioned on the road to Damascus (Acts 26:14). However, there is no record of Barnabas ever reminding Paul of his
past. What a great example for leaders!

Looking out over the Sunday morning
congregation, Pastor Al noticed that for the
third Sunday in a row the Petersons were
not in their usual spot. He had walked Mary
and Tom, the parents of this family of five,
through a difficult time of restoration in
their marriage after Mary's confession of infidelity. His visit to
their home the next week confirmed his fear that they were at-
tending another church. The couple held hands as Tom struggled
to answer the pastor's request for an explanation. "Well, Pastor Al,
the truth is, we are so grateful for all that you and the Lord have
done for us. We tried so hard, but it just seemed that you never
looked at us, never talked to us the same afterward."

> Generous mercy
> givers learn to
> drop forgiven sins
> into God's sea of
> forgetfulness.

Generous mercy givers learn to drop forgiven sins into God's
sea of forgetfulness.

Honor. Finally, strong leaders can be generous in bestowing honor to those who work with them. The more honor you give away, the more your own reservoir grows.

Jesus honored Nathanael, calling him a "true Israelite in whom there is no guile" (John 1:47). He honored a poor widow's offering (Mark 12:42–44). And the Master honored Mary Magdalene's loving act of anointing Him for His burial: "Truly, I say to you, wherever this gospel is proclaimed in the whole world, what she has done will also be told in memory of her" (Matt. 26:13).

Yet it is difficult for some leaders to honor those they work with. Actress and singer Barbra Streisand's infamous words in her acceptance speech for the 1969 Best Actress Oscar marked her forever. She said that "she would like to 'thank all the little people' behind her victory. Not surprisingly, the backhanded compliment didn't sit well with the 'little people' in the unions who worked on the film."[17] Cutting off the flow of honor makes you smaller.

I believe the difficulty comes from two polar extremes. Self-pride blinds leaders to the important part others play in their success. On the other hand, leaders who struggle with low self-esteem issues often fear that building up another will tear them down. A clear sign of that battle is giving words of praise but quickly following them with a joke or a cutting remark, knowingly or unknowingly decreasing the positive effect of the encouragement.

I don't remember my error, but I will never forget a moment of correction I experienced as a young soldier from the chaplain I worked for. "Isaac, I used to say that you were the best chaplain's assistant in Germany, but after this I can no longer say that." Whatever his intention may have been, his comment left me confused and hurt. I determined that I would never put another person through the same experience.

Honor those who helped you succeed, and celebrate others' successes. Stop yourself when tempted to throw a shadow on their limelight. Terry and I decided that a major part of our church planting program would include celebrating birthdays, anniversaries, new convert baptisms, church dedications—anything we could do to honor the families who had launched themselves into growing the Kingdom with us.

I have discovered a powerful phrase that almost invariably breaks through the typical everyday interaction with those around us. After receiving good service from someone such as a waiter or a representative on the phone, I ask the person's name. I then call him or her by name and ask, "Has anyone told you what a great job you are doing today?" Invariably, the person will stop and think for a moment before responding, "No, not today." I come back with, "Be encouraged!" Those few words almost always bring a reaction, ranging from a smile to the tears of one cashier who was having a terrible day at work. Proverbs 18:21 declares that death and life are in the power of the tongue. As much as is in me, I will sow life into the lives of those around me.

Barnabas had a generous spirit. He invested years of his life into Paul. In all their time together, we never read that he brought up Paul's past persecution of the church. That was biblical mercy in action. Barnabas' actions honored his fellow missionary, including Paul in all that he did. If you want to have a powerful impact as a leader, there are few better examples you can follow.

Wrong

When Cephas came to Antioch, I (Paul) opposed him to his face... even Barnabas was carried away with their hypocrisy

Barnabas nudged Peter under the table as Paul walked over. Barnabas recognized the look in his friend's eyes, penetrating and focused. Peter looked up and smiled. "Paul, join us!" he urged.

"Join you?!" It was not a question. Paul's voice was loud enough to be heard by the other visitors from Jerusalem. "How can I join you when you separate yourselves from our Gentile brothers and sisters? How can you live like a Gentile till your friends from home show up? Is the body of Christ thus divided?" Conversation over the evening meal fell to an ominous silence.

"And Barnabas, my friend, are you being carried along with them as well?" Paul's rebuke made Barnabas wince. He was right. Of course, he was right! The visiting brothers from Jerusalem had no understanding of the months the two of them had worked side by side in ministry, their lives in danger, discipling and loving people who were in every way brothers and sisters in Christ, just not Jews. The meeting in Jerusalem should have solved the problem, but it was hard to change attitudes that had guided people for a lifetime.

Paul turned on his heel and went back to the group of Antiochan believers who were breaking bread together across the room. The food in Barnabas' mouth suddenly tasted like sand. He shared a pained look with Peter, while the others seated on the crude benches around the table shifted uncomfortably. The awkwardness of the moment lay heavily on everyone like a rain-soaked woolen blanket.

111

Barnabas stood. "Excuse me, brothers," he mumbled, heading for the door. He couldn't stay at the table, but he couldn't yet bring himself to join Paul. So he walked out into the coolness of the evening.

"Father, forgive me," he began, then stopped as thoughts and memories overwhelmed him. The people around the table had been his friends from the beginning. The whole issue of the Gentile believers was so difficult. The Messiah came to Israel. All the apostles were Jewish. Yet Jesus had commanded them to carry the good news to all the world.

And what about Paul? Once again, his companion had placed himself at the center of controversy. But he was right! "Oh, God, help me!" Barnabas cried in his heart. As he stood quietly in the dark, images of their trips to and from Asia Minor, to Jerusalem, and again to Antioch played repeatedly in his mind.

He couldn't straddle the line any longer. How could he feel so old and like a rebuked child at the same time? Yet he knew what he had to do.

Finally, Barnabas took a deep breath, turned, and headed back inside. He hesitated, then slowly walked over to Paul's table and sat down. Paul regarded his companion briefly, his eyes now calm, and handed him a piece of bread.

(Based on Galatians 2:11–14)

Admitting you are wrong is a difficult task for anyone to do. I still remember my dad's often repeated joke: "I was wrong once. Well, I thought that I was wrong, but I was actually right!"

Jewish believers in Christ struggled with a cultural identity that was based on observing the rite of circumcision, the laws of Moses, and the traditions of their elders. These firmly held beliefs meant that Jews didn't associate with Gentiles, and breaking through that cultural barrier was difficult. In Acts 6, the church appointed seven deacons because believing Jewish widows were given preference over their Gentile counterparts. Peter needed the vision of the unclean animals in the sheets before he would bring the gospel to the household of Cornelius, the Roman centurion, in Acts 10. And still he struggled, as did Barnabas.

Admitting mistakes and errors open vulnerabilities that some leaders may not want to face. Will those who follow you think less of you when they see your fallible side? Will you lose influence with them?

I was with a group of national and area church leaders looking up at the sagging roof on a church I was in charge of building. I had tried an unproven system of wooden trusses to carry the roof's weight over the twenty-five-foot span between the sanctuary walls. It didn't work. The force of the sagging roof had bowed out the block walls and cracked the concrete support columns. I wondered where my mistake would leave me standing in the eyes of those whose respect and trust I needed to continue with our church planting projects.

My greatest error was not the roof system but an irrational belief that my value as a leader depended on the image of my own infallibility. Some leaders work hard to build an image of strength, intelligence, and competence that becomes the basis for their position. However, your selection as a leader is probably not because you are the strongest, the smartest, or the best at what you do. If it were, you would be forced to continually try to prove your qualifications, much like gunfighters in the old American West felt they had to duel with anyone who was thought to be better.

> The energy and time spent to maintain an image means less energy and time to address a problem.

The desire to protect this kind of image can lead to one of several negative responses to mistakes or problems.

1 Deny. Some leaders try to deny or minimize errors. Supervisor Tom had the habit of postponing or cancelling meetings that threatened to touch on the diminishing sales figures in his department. Rather than dealing with her husband's drinking problem, Darla called into work to tell her husband's boss that he was sick.

2 Scapegoat. Other leaders look for someone or something to blame. The scapegoat concept comes from the Old Testament practice of releasing a live goat into the desert after confessing the people's sins over its head (Lev. 16:22). The goat carried the sins of the people, releasing them from the punishment for their actions. In the same way, leaders will blame an absent team member, unfavorable circumstances, or anything else to keep from dealing with the reality of a mistake or problem.

3 Attack. The force and emotion of a verbal attack will often deflect attention from underlying problems. Ryan, the children's pastor, was called into the senior pastor's office to explain why transportation was not available to bring kids back after their week at summer camp. But rather than read the e-mails Ryan brought to show that he had requested the vans the week before, the pastor ranted for fifteen minutes about how bad Ryan had made him look and how this was a poor demonstration of leadership skills on Ryan's part.

The energy and time spent to maintain an image means less energy and time to address a problem. And like a spinning top that begins to wobble, it gets harder and harder to maintain that false image. Sooner or later it will fall.

Your greatest battles are always fought and won between your ears. Salvation in Christ begins with recognizing that you need a Savior, acknowledging that your current path is wrong and needs a change. Reaching the point of admitting a mistake begins inside you. And the good news is that once you admit a mistake, an error, or a problem to yourself, you open the door to a solution, whether that be as eternal as the future of your soul or as temporal as a church roof.

> Taking responsibility builds confidence and trust with those who work with you

Take responsibility. As I stood with the Uruguayan leaders looking up at the sagging roof, I realized there was no way around it, no quick fix to this one. "Esta es mi responsibilidad. Yo lo corrijo. This is my responsibility, I will make it right," I told them, although I had no clue how that was going to happen or even what had to be done. I waited for their comments and criticism, but none came. The leaders looked around a little more before walking to their cars.

Looking back on that moment now, I believe that as good leaders they were looking for solutions and took my assumption of responsibility as the first step in finding one. It became an important lesson to me. President Harry Truman was known for a small sign on his Oval Office desk that said, "The Buck Stops Here." The phrase comes from a ritual in card games in which a marker or "buck"—often an actual buckhorn knife—was passed to each player when it was his or her turn to deal. The phrase *passing the buck* came to mean refusing to deal or be responsible. If the buck stopped at your spot, you were responsible. President Truman's sign meant that, in the end, he was responsible for the decisions of his administration.[18]

The first step in assuming responsibility may be as simple as saying, "I'm sorry." One of our children called me while I was writing this chapter. I read them the story about Barnabas that accompanies this chapter and talked about what I wanted to say. Their response surprised and gratified me. "You know, Dad, one thing you and Mom taught us well was how to apologize."

Apologies, spoken or not, can be powerful. German chancellor Willy Brandt left witnesses and the world awestruck in 1970 when he spontaneously knelt on the steps of the monument to the Warsaw Ghetto Uprising where nearly half a million Jews died during World War II. "There was no doubt about it, Willy Brandt surprised everyone. Communist politicians in Poland at the time were astonished by the brief gesture. Polish intellectuals, however, have highly revered Willy Brandt ever since."[19]

Taking responsibility builds confidence and trust with those who work with you—confidence that they can come to you and trust that you will listen and do something about their concerns. Think for a moment about the people you deeply trust. If you were to bring them an error or problem that needs to be addressed, how would they respond to you? More than likely, your trust comes from the confidence that they would take responsibility and do something to help.

Take action. Five thousand dollars. That was the projected cost of removing the defective roof and trusses and replacing them with steel trusses and a metal roof. I prayed, called one of our faithful donors, and later thanked the Lord for His faithfulness in helping us fix the roof. That church has since grown and is reaching their community with the good news of Jesus Christ. I doubt that many people glance up at the ceiling and remember the mistake that almost brought the roof down on their building, but I remember and so do those leaders who stood there that day with me.

However, far too many churches, projects, and wonderful ideas have languished and often died for the lack of taking necessary and often promised steps to solve a problem or remove an obstacle. Few things are more frustrating for coworkers or volunteers than watching that happen.

"These don't look like ants." Liana pointed to the tiny insects that lay dead on their wooden window sill. "Ok, who should we call?" her husband, Carl, replied, still not very concerned. Two phone calls and a pest treatment later, both Liana and Carl were concerned but relieved. The termites that had invaded from the front lawn and begun their destructive march through the couple's home were stopped before doing any real damage. Carl's sister and brother-in-law had a much more expensive story to tell. Untreated termite damage to their home had cost them thousands of dollars, forcing them to replace parts of a wall, floor joists, and the header over their garage door.

If not dealt with, problems, errors, and misunderstandings eat away at relationships and trust just like termites. The sooner they are identified and acted upon, the greater the chance of minimal or no damage.

Many times, lack of action is not due to lack of motivation but rather to lack of a concrete plan of action. Consider the steps you need to take to correct the problem. Who else needs to be involved? How will you know the problem has been solved?

Take steps to move on. Moving on means not letting your past sins and errors control your future decisions. When we talked about dealing with failure, I highlighted the importance of not allowing failure to become the last chapter of your life. One of the greatest failures everyone struggles with is the failure to live in the light of God's forgiveness.

Forgiveness is the foundation of our lives in Jesus Christ. Saul became the great apostle Paul because he experienced the miracle of forgiveness for persecuting the church and causing the deaths of many Christians. He acknowledged that in his writings and did not live in the shadow of his sin. "There is therefore now no condemnation for those who are in Christ Jesus" (Rom. 8:1) begins a Scripture passage that shines brightly as a pinnacle reflecting the fullness of God's grace to us.

The Scriptures don't show us Barnabas' response to Paul's confrontation over the issue of eating with the Gentile believers, but the attitude of taking responsibility, action, and steps to move on fits well with what we do see of his personality.

Transparently acknowledge your mistakes and sins, ask forgiveness, and do what you can to make everything right. Then, under God's grace, move on to the next challenge that lies before you. Those who work with you will be impacted by your decision. And some may thank you.

Conflict

There arose a sharp disagreement, so that they separated from each other. Barnabas took Mark with him and sailed away to Cyprus

"No!" Paul's sharp response brought Barnabas up short. Barnabas looked his friend in the eyes. The same unbreakable stare he knew so well met his gaze.

A few days ago, Paul had suggested they return to visit the churches established on their first trip. "That's a great idea, Paul," Barnabas had responded. "What would you think of taking Mark with us again?"

"Let's pray about it," Paul had replied. But his brusque tone warned Barnabas that he did not favor the suggestion.

As Barnabas prayed, he became convinced that Mark needed another chance, more time working with the two apostles to take him to the next step in his own ministry.

Later, when Barnabas broached the subject again, Paul seemed exasperated. "Barnabas, you know the dangers we will face. We cannot afford to take a chance that Mark will leave us again."

"But I can see it! He's grown and just needs another opportunity."

"Well, my brother, let me pray again tonight, and we can talk again in the morning."

Barnabas had run into his cousin that night after the evening prayers with the church leaders of Antioch. "What did he say, Barnabas?" the young man had asked.

"We will reach a decision tomorrow," the apostle had replied. Seeing the alarm on Mark's face, he continued, "But

119

don't worry. I have peace about this. I know the Lord will guide us all."

That peace made this moment extremely difficult. What was the Lord doing? What was Paul thinking? Barnabas looked again at the man he had taken under his wing, taught, and empowered. How could they be so far apart? Barnabas knew he had to make one last point to his former disciple. "Do you remember our trip back to Antioch from Tarsus?" he asked.

Paul's look darkened. "How could you bring that up now? Are you going to obligate me because of your obedience to the Lord years ago?!"

"It's the same!" Barnabas shot back.

"No, it's not!" Paul countered.

Then Barnabas knew what he had to do, just as surely as he had known about Paul when they first met. He met Paul's stony gaze with one of his own. "I will take John Mark and sail to Cyprus."

Paul broke the intervening silence in a low but firm tone. "Then I will ask Silas to go with me to Syria and Cilicia."

Grieved yet still at peace, Barnabas watched as Paul turned his back and walked away.

(Based on Acts 15:36–41)

Conflict can be defined as "a disagreement between two or more people who perceive a threat against their goals, needs, or desires." If you are in leadership, you will face conflict. It is said that as much as 30 percent of a leader's time is spent managing people problems. Effective leaders learn the best ways to deal with and resolve conflict.

> If you are in leadership, you will face conflict.

While we don't know much about the way Barnabas handled conflict, we can see Paul's approach in Acts and his Epistles. From persecuting Christians to later confronting Peter about his treatment of the Gentiles, Paul attacked problems head on. His confrontational style with the Grecian Jews in Jerusalem led to his being sent to Tarsus. That same style led to Bar-Jesus losing his sight in Cyprus.

The opposite way to deal with conflict is to ignore or deny it. Denial is a powerful coping mechanism that can help a person get through a difficult situation. But ignoring problems will not make them go away. Harold and Penney worked with an administrative assistant who constantly caused problems with their young adults' group. Their response was to deal with each problem as it came up instead of confronting the assistant's detrimental behaviors. They were afraid that confronting him would cause greater problems.

Other leaders try to accommodate everyone in dealing with conflict. Some take that approach to an extreme and become like a chameleon that changes colors to match its surroundings. Peter's behavior could be described this way. When Jewish believers from Jerusalem visited the Antioch church, Peter shunned the people he had previously fellowshipped with. The night Jesus was brought before His accusers, Peter denied Christ using the coarse language of those who stood around the fire with him.

Still others negotiate, looking for everyone to compromise a little to arrive at a mutually acceptable solution. Like sellers and buyers of a house, the result is not necessarily what either party started out wanting, but all walk away with something.

A final style of handling conflict is collaboration, which involves seeking to help everyone work together so that all achieve their goals. In this process, individuals lay down their personal needs and goals to work toward a common goal. In Acts 6, seven men were selected to collaborate to meet the needs of the entire body of Christ regardless of their own feelings about the Jewish and Gentile widows.

The way a person handles conflict may vary depending on the circumstance. Henry was a mid-level supervisor for an auto manufacturer as well as a board member at his church. One day, his supervisor at work called him in for a meeting to discuss why productions goals were not met the previous two months.

As usual, Henry was contrite at the meeting. He tended to avoid conflicts with his supervisor at any cost, conceding any point necessary to do so. However, that evening, Henry attended a church board meeting to discuss a decrease in church attendance and offerings. There, as he often did, Henry aggressively argued his point of view, regardless of what others thought or said. Henry had little influence at his job but enjoyed considerable sway on the church board. His two leadership positions brought out different facets of his vulnerability and weak sense of worth.

You can improve your own role as a team player and leader simply by recognizing the way you handle conflict. One way you can do that is to consider two distinct scenarios: Are you on the receiving end of conflict, or do you need to deal with a problem and perhaps initiate a potential conflict?

Conflict directed at you. Terry and I had just returned from an overseas trip when I received a voice mail from a supervisor who stated that no matter what happened, he supported me. The only problem was that I had no idea what had happened to warrant his supportive call! A quick check of my e-mails revealed a scathing complaint registered against me that had been sent to my supervisor as well as to his superior. As Terry and I worked our way through this conflict, I was reminded of some important principles that apply to most problems and conflicts.

> Warranted or not, what feels like a personal attack may reveal a kernel of truth.

1 They don't demand an instant response. A quick answer is not usually well thought through. Taking time to discuss the problem with your spouse and trusted friends will help. I thank the Lord for the sound advice I received in dealing with that conflict.

2 They are often not just baseless attacks. Warranted or not, what feels like a personal attack may reveal a kernel of truth. After thinking long and hard about the complaint, my response to my supervisor was, "When you take the heat out of the e-mail, there is a point to what the writer says." The more time you spend defending your position, the less you will have to deal with the immediate crisis and perhaps any underlying problems.

3 They are not solved by counterattacks. Many conflicts become lures to draw you away from the primary goal of dealing with the problem. It requires inner strength and confidence to avoid distractions, no matter how important they may appear to be at the time. I once got into a rock fight with my childhood best friend, Charlie Morris. It all started on the way home from school with a few pebbles tossed back and forth but ended with my head split open—only because Charlie had better aim than I did! One way to stop a rock fight is to stop throwing rocks! Eventually, the other side will run out of ammunition. And don't save any rocks for later use.

4 They should be dealt with and left behind. Sometimes it is impossible to completely correct a situation or restore a relationship. In the midst of a powerful passage on Christian living in Romans 12, Paul gives us a pearl of an answer to that dilemma: "If possible, so far as it depends on you, live peaceably with all" (v. 18). You can control only your own feelings and actions. Do what you need to do for your part: apologize, change a behavior—whatever is necessary. There is no guarantee that the other party will change, but that is in God's hands. In my case, I never reacted or responded directly to the complainant. I just did what I needed to do to resolve the issue that had prompted the complaint.

5 They can become points of growth if you allow them to. This conflict led me to prayer, consultation, and lots of thought. The Lord taught me to trust in Him on a whole new level, and I came out with a new sense of self-confidence.

Conflict initiated by you. Have you ever wondered what went through Nathan's mind as he walked through the palace on his way to confront David's sin with Bathsheba? The prophet obviously put a lot of thought into his conversation. He came up with the story of the rich man who took the poor man's lamb. He must have wondered about King David's response to the conflict that arose from his declaration, "You are the man!" David could have imprisoned or even killed Nathan, but he didn't (2 Sam. 12:1–14).

Positive conflict resolution that you initiate requires good preparation. Here are some ideas that may help in resolving conflicts.

1 Start with a specific goal. What do you want to accomplish as a result of your meeting? For example, "As a result of talking to Harold, I would like to see him treat his coworkers with more respect."

2 Speak from your own perspective instead of the other person's. "You need to ..." becomes "I feel ... when I see ..."

3 Be specific and avoid generalizations. "You never come in on time ..." becomes "I noticed that you were late last Tuesday and Thursday."

4 Address present behaviors instead of the past. Don't yield to the temptation of adding, "That reminds me of last year when you ..."

5 Avoid insults and words that cause hurt. Don't use statements like, "You know that was a very dumb decision on your part."

6 Don't look to punish or get back at the person. Remarks like "I have half a mind to fire you for that" will usually build resentment more than bring change.

7 Don't judge motives. Saying, "It just looks to me that you don't like working here" isn't helpful. Accept what the person tells you at face value.

8 Set workable solutions, not winning, as the goal. Avoid saying, "We aren't leaving here until you admit that you were wrong," or "You need to apologize to your coworkers for your attitude."

Proverbs 27:17 instructs us that "iron sharpens iron, and one man sharpens another." Sparks fly and a loud scraping sound is given off. But the intent is to provide a fine cutting edge on a sword or a spear so it will accomplish the purpose for which it was designed. Purposeful and properly managed conflict can achieve the same end.

Paul and Barnabas' sharp conflict led to the end of a partnership that had accomplished many things for the Lord. While both continued, worked with new companions, and saw new victories in the Kingdom, we will never know what might have happened if they had resolved their differences in a biblical manner. Do all you can not only to avoid conflict (that just won't happen) but also to deal with conflict in a healthy way. Doing so will mark you as a dependable leader who is not afraid to face and resolve conflict.

Legacy

Get Mark and bring him with you, for he is very useful to me for ministry

Mark ducked his head to miss the low stone ceiling as he passed through the dark entrance, his eyes slowly adjusting to the gloom of the poorly lit cell. The smell of unwashed bodies and urine hung heavily in the air. Mark couldn't see the opposite wall, but the room felt oppressive. "Paul?" he called in a voice that quickly died without an echo. He caught movement in the shadows and heard a voice he instantly recognized.

"Timothy, my son?"

"No Brother Paul. It's me, John Mark. Timothy is arranging our lodging, but I wanted to come right over to see you."

"Ah, Mark! I wasn't sure you would come," replied the bald and stooped old man. Mark squinted in the darkness, trying to make out the apostle who stood before him. He did not look well, and the chain around his ankle jerked against his leg, a reminder from the guard just around the corner not to stray too far.

Both men stood for an awkward moment until Mark reached out to hug Paul tightly. With tears in his eyes, Mark whispered, "He's gone!"

Paul pulled back slightly to look him in the eye. "Barnabas?"

"Yes," Mark began. "We were back, preaching in Salamis ..."

Paul interrupted, "His hometown. He never could stay away for long. You remember how Barnabas took us there first when we landed in Cyprus. And he took you back there when we, when we ..."

127

"Parted ways. Yes, I remember," Mark supplied, feeling no bitterness. "God had given us several new believers to disciple, but the Jews caught Barnabas out alone one evening and stoned him." He paused and swallowed. "I found him on the outskirts of the city and buried him near the grove of olive trees where he loved to pray."

Silence reigned for several moments.

Finally, Paul cleared his throat and said, "Tell me about your new work."

Mark answered, "It's almost finished, but it's nothing like your letters. I've been traveling with Peter and pulling together the stories and the teachings of the Master."

"Ah, Mark," the apostle responded, nodding his approval. "I'm sure the Holy Spirit breathes upon you as you write. It's been—what?—more than thirty years since Jesus returned to heaven. The churches need a faithful record of all the Master said and did."

Silence fell between them again. Mark continued to study the old man before him, wondering what had prompted Paul to summon him.

Perhaps sensing his questions, Paul began, "Mark, I was wrong to have opposed your coming with us." Mark waved his hand in protest, but the apostle continued, "You are useful for the ministry. You are useful to me, and I should have told you long ago." Mark nodded his thanks, not sure what to say.

Paul paused before asking, "Where will you go now?"

"The Lord has opened a door for ministry in Alexandria. I will travel there as soon as the weather permits," Mark replied. He hesitated, then said, "Timothy tells me that with this second imprisonment you may not ..." His voice trailed away.

Paul's rough hand, callused from years of tent making, grasped the back of Mark's neck in affection. Mark recognized the same penetrating intensity in the older man's eyes that Barnabas had known so well. "I have fought the good fight. I have kept the faith!" Paul's declaration was unwavering.

The chain jerked again, signaling the end of Mark's visit for that day. Yet Paul's gaze continued to focus on the younger man as he added, "Barnabas kept the faith as well. He saw something in me. He saw something in you. He did not give up on either of us."

Mark watched silently as Paul slowly turned and disappeared into the darkness of the cell.

(Based on 2 Timothy 4:11 and early church tradition)

Temple of Praise Church was known in the 1980s as one of the first megachurches in the region. Pastor Caleb put the congregation on the cutting edge of church ministry. Hundreds of believers drove many miles to attend Sunday services at the church, and Pastor Caleb came to be in demand across the country as a speaker.

Suddenly, one day it was over. Pastor Caleb announced from the pulpit that he felt led to leave the church to focus on his national ministry. Almost immediately, attendance began to drop, and before long all that remained of the congregation was a tiny group that made the main sanctuary feel and sound cavernous. The investigation into the fire that later destroyed the building revealed no foul play, but some thought it a convenient coincidence. Pastor Caleb's influence in that area lasted as long as the ashes from the fire that scattered in the wind.

> The true impact of your leadership will not be seen until after you are gone.

The true impact of your leadership will not be seen until after you are gone. Influential leaders keep that in mind in everything they do during their tenure as leaders.

After his heated disagreement with Paul, Barnabas disappeared from the pages of the New Testament. Yet even in taking Silas with him to southern Turkey, Paul followed the pattern for ministry that Barnabas had laid down. Barnabas' influence lasted, and his legacy still carries on today.

Consider these suggestions for having a lasting impact as a leader.

Plan ahead. The rock music world was shaken to learn that megastar Prince died suddenly of a drug overdose, leaving no will behind to dispose of his estimated 300-million-dollar estate. It will take the courts years to sort out what to do with his wealth, which included a mansion and hundreds of unpublished songs.[20] Prince gave no thought to those who would manage his rock empire after he was gone.

During His three years of active ministry, Jesus constantly talked about the fact that He would not always be with His disciples. Their job would be to establish and grow the church based on Jesus' teachings. Christ also promised that He would send them another comforter, the Holy Spirit (John 14:6).

Strong legacies don't happen by accident. Ask yourself what would happen if you were suddenly taken out of the picture. Could someone step in, not just to cover, but to carry on the vision you have laid out? If not, what would it take on your part to make that a reality? Just as thoughtful parents spend time and money preparing a will to spare their children confusion, pain, and possible conflict, strong leaders prepare for the time that they step away from their position of influence.

Over the ten years of Pastor Phil's leadership, the church he pastored had purchased property and had completed three phases of construction as the congregation grew and thrived. However, for the past two years, Phil had been feeling from the Lord that his pastorate was nearing an end. During that time, Phil talked this change over with the church board, his state overseer, and a few trusted pastor friends. When God later confirmed to Phil that the time had come to relinquish his pastorate at the church, his letter of resignation came as no surprise to the leadership of the church and of the state. He had done all he could do to prepare himself, the other leaders, and his congregation for the coming transition.

Recognize when it's time to leave. I believe one cause of the conflict between Paul and Barnabas was that Barnabas did not recognize his time with Paul had come to an end. Barnabas wanted Paul to continue with him and make the same kind of investment in Mark that Barnabas had made in Paul. His perspective was different from Paul's because he could see something in Mark that Paul couldn't see. It was a hallmark of Barnabas' ministry, but Paul's strengths were in different areas.

What are some indicators that the time has come to consider making a change?

1 You have a new vision. I can still relive the moment I stood in the first set of bleachers at a conference, holding my four-year-old daughter in my arms, when God called us to be missionaries. Based on that call, Terry and I resigned our pastorate to start a brand-new life.

2 You have accomplished what you set out to do. In Uruguay, after ten years of Bible school ministry, Terry and I felt called to plant ten new churches. As we drew near the end of that goal, I began to feel stirrings in my heart that it was time for another change.

3 Those who work with you are ready to take on more responsibility, perhaps some of yours. It can be very threatening when someone working with you begins to do some of the things you have done. However, it can also be a sign that he or she is ready to do more.

4 Your passion tank is empty. Ex-CEO of General Electric Jack Welch identifies five essential qualities of leadership: personal positive energy, the ability to energize others, an edge to make tough calls, the talent to execute, and passion. Note that three of these have to do with energy and passion.[21] Lack of passion leads to stagnation. When you think more about past victories than future challenges, it may be time for a change.

Don't leave surprises behind. A good friend moved his family into their newly purchased home during the winter, only to have the furnace completely go out after just a few days. A careful inspection revealed that the furnace and the duct system needed to be replaced at a high cost. The previous owner had made quick repairs to a serious problem that soon demanded the new owner's attention. It was a very unwelcome surprise.

Do everything possible to deal with problems, finish projects, and clearly inform those who follow you about the situations they might face. If possible, speak to your successor or leave him or her detailed notes. The new leader may or may not follow your recommendations for dealing with situations, but at the very least he or she will have the needed information to move forward. Your church, mission, or project can continue to grow depending on what you leave behind.

Build bridges instead of burning them. One of the saddest stories about leadership transition is found in the first few verses of 1 Kings 2. Just before King David died, he commanded young Solomon to kill Joab and Shimei. Joab was David's cousin and general over his army but had used his position to manipulate David on several occasions. Shimei had called down curses on David when he fled the coup led by Absalom. Both had done wrong to David, and the old king wanted vengeance brought on them.

> Do everything possible to deal with problems, finish projects, and clearly inform those who follow you about the situations they might face.

How different from the example of Joseph in Genesis! Joseph's brothers feared that after their father, Jacob, passed away, Joseph would seek revenge for being sold into slavery. Yet Joseph repeated three words in Genesis 50:19 and 21 that set the pattern for successful transitions: "Do not fear."

Enable those who follow you to build on what you have done without fear that you will exact payment for past mistakes, disagreements, or even attacks against you. Forgiveness is a powerful tool. Forgive, not on the basis of whether it is deserved, but on how it can build a bridge between your work and your successors' work.

Let go. Our family home was only half a block from the church that we pastored, and it took over a year for our house to sell after we resigned our pastorate to begin our missionary career. It was so difficult to refer our parishioners—our friends—back to the new pastor and state leaders when they came to us looking for counsel for problems at the church, but we held fast. We were no longer their pastors.

I do not subscribe to the thought that once you leave a leadership position, whether a pastorate or another place of responsibility, you should cut off all contact with former colleagues and friends. Terry and I still have many friends from the church we pastored and from our work in Uruguay. However, there must be a clear line of demarcation between friendship and leadership. That can be worked out in several ways.

1 **Expect changes to the way you did things.** There will be changes, and you may or may not approve of them.

2 **Avoid giving suggestions unless asked by the leader who replaces you.** Most likely, your replacement will make mistakes that you can easily foresee. Yet that leader will need to learn just as you did.

3 **Never, never criticize those who take your place.** Jesus' words in John 8:7 fit well here: "Let the sinless one cast the first stone." You made your mistakes along the way. Let your successor deal with his or her own challenges without having to worry about you.

I believe your legacy is built over the time you serve as a leader, from the day you begin until the day you turn in your keys. Love the Lord. Serve your people. Encourage others. See what others don't see, and do what others won't do. Then leave well. If you do that, your legacy will rise on its own and remain like a fine perfume that hangs in the air long after its wearer leaves the room.

Terry and I were humbled by feedback we received after we left Uruguay. A leader had returned from an international church planting meeting and told me, "As national leaders discussed church planting, your name never came up, but I could see your fingerprints on everything they shared." Today, the national church continues its emphasis on church planting. We are gone, but new leaders have arisen to accept the call and challenge of reaching Uruguay with the good news of Jesus Christ.

Paul never mentioned Barnabas' name after they parted ways, yet the older apostle's fingerprints were all over both Paul's and Mark's work. In fact, I believe that after Jesus Christ, Barnabas is the most influential leader of the New Testament, and the sweet fragrance of his influence continues to arise every time someone reads his story.

Conclusion

The Barnabas Way is a journey. Barnabas' journey began with his faith in God and an open heart that grew into the leadership principles that marked his ministry. Barnabas developed those principles as he traveled from his home in Cyprus to Jerusalem, to Antioch, to Tarsus, back to Cyprus, and then to Asia Minor and invested himself in two struggling future leaders.

Barnabas saw in Paul and Mark what others did not see. The greatest accomplishments in the Kingdom always begin with a glimpse of what could be better, what someone might be able to do, or perhaps what God might do.

Barnabas' vision propelled him to do what others would not do. He took those young men under his wing and walked alongside them as they grew. Barnabas empowered and released both men to go far beyond what Barnabas was able to do alone.

And Barnabas paid a price that others would not pay. He took the risk to work with young Saul, something the apostles would not do. Later, he left Paul's side to start the whole process again with John Mark.

It wasn't easy; it certainly wasn't perfect. There were miracles and disasters, challenges and conflict. Barnabas made mistakes just like you and I do. But oh, what a ride was this journey called the Barnabas Way! In the end Barnabas helped to shape two principal writers of the New Testament, both of whom became recognized leaders in the early church.

Paul followed Barnabas' example and invited many young leaders to walk with him on his own journey of building the Kingdom. Silas, Luke, Timothy, Titus, Philemon, Lydia, and many others emerge in the book of Acts and Paul's Epistles, forming an unbroken chain that reaches through the years to you and me.

I challenge you on your own journey. Consider the principles of this book in light of your own thoughts and experiences. Take what you need, leave behind what doesn't work for you, but don't be too quick to avoid the things that may make you uncomfortable.

Then be a Barnabas! Many young Sauls, John Marks, Timothys, and others are waiting for a Barnabas to walk alongside them as they develop their own leadership skills. Your influence could have a life-changing impact on them.

Or perhaps you need a Barnabas to come alongside and help mold you into a better vessel for use in the Kingdom. Ask the Lord to send a Barnabas into your life, then be open. One may come looking for you.

And so it continues—the Barnabas Way.

Endnotes

1   Martin Luther King Jr., "I've Been to the Mountaintop" (speech, Memphis, TN, April 3, 1968), 6. *A Call to Conscience: The Landmark Speeches of Dr. Martin Luther King Jr.,* accessed October 17, 2017, http://kingencyclopedia.stanford.edu/kingweb/publications/speeches/I've_been_to_the_mountaintop.pdf

2   Martin Luther King Jr., "I've Been to the Mountaintop" (speech, Memphis, TN, April 3, 1968), 6. *A Call to Conscience: The Landmark Speeches of Dr. Martin Luther King Jr.,* accessed October 17, 2017,

3   Suzy Platt, ed., *Respectfully Quoted: A Dictionary of Quotations, requested from the Congressional Research Service* (Washington DC: Library of Congress, 1989; Bartleby.com, 2003), accessed October 26, 2017, http://www.bartleby.com/73/465.html

4   Today I Found Out, "The Can Opener Wasn't Invented until 48 Years after the Invention of the Can," June 4, 2012, accessed October 30, 2017, http://www.todayifoundout.com/index.php/2012/06/the-can-opener-wasnt-invented-until-48-years-after-the-invention-of-the-can/

5   David McCullough, *The Path between the Seas: The Creation of the Panama Canal, 1870–1914* (New York: Simon & Schuster, 2004), Kindle edition.

6   Donald W. McCullough, *Waking from the American Dream: Growing through Your Disappointments* (Downers Grove, IL: InterVarsity Press, 1988), 181.

7   Kendall and Starla Bridges, *Better Marriage: Against All Odds* (Carrollton, TX: Kendall Bridges Ministries, 2016), 106.

8   "Jerry Rice," Wikipedia, last modified August 19, 2017. Accessed August 21, 2017. https://en.wikipedia.org/wiki/Jerry_Rice

9   Malcolm Gladwell, *Outliers: The Story of Success* (New York: Little, Brown and Company, 2008), 39.

10   "Eddie 'The Eagle' Edwards," Wikipedia, last modified October 23, 2017. Accessed November 2, 2017. https://en.wikipedia.org/wiki/Eddie_%22The_Eagle%22_Edwards

11   Jack Busch, "Hard Work in 5 Easy Steps: Understanding Perseverance in the Modern Age," *Primer Magazine*, 2012. Accessed August 21, 2017. http://www.primermagazine.com/2012/live/what-is-hard-work

12   Ibid.

13   Libby Kane, "Mrs. Fields Cookies: How Debbi Fields Built an Empire from Scratch." Accessed August 21, 2017. https://www.themuse.com/advice/mrs-fields-cookies-how-debbi-fields-built-an-empire-from-scratch

14   *The Man Who Stopped the Desert,* directed by Mark Dodd, 2009. Accessed August 22, 2017. http://www.1080films.co.uk/downloads/man-who-stopped-the-desert-info-pack.pdf

15   C. S. Lewis, *The Chronicles of Narnia: The Lion, the Witch and the Wardrobe* (New York: Scholastic, 1995), 92.

16   Paige Levin, *Maryland Officer Buys Diapers for Mother Caught Stealing Them,* CNN, July 27, 2017. Accessed August 23, 2017. http://www.cnn.com/2017/07/27/us/cop-buys-diapers-trnd/index.html

17   Kirk Baird, "Pushing the Envelope: Oscar Winners Famous for Memorable Acceptance Speeches," Las Vegas Sun, February 23, 2004. Accessed August 23, 2017.

18   Atkins, Alexander. "Tag Archives: Origin of the Buck Stops Here." *Bookshelf* (blog). March 12, 2013. Accessed September 11, 2017. https://atkinsbookshelf.wordpress.com/tag/origin-of-the-buck-stops-here/

19   DW. "7.12.1970: Willy Brandt Falls to His Knees." *Today in History.* Accessed September 11, 2017. http://www.today-in-history.de/index.php?what=thmanu&manu_id=1668&tag=7&monat=12&year=2015&dayisset=1&lang=en

20   Lisa Respers France, Stephanie Elam, Jason Kravarik, and Dave Goldman, "Prince Had No Will, Says His Sister," CNN Money, April 26, 2016. Accessed August 23, 2017. http://money.cnn.com/2016/04/26/news/companies/prince-no-will/

21   Welch, Jack. "Former GE CEO Jack Welch Says Leaders Have 5 Basic Traits—And Only 2 Can Be Taught." *Business Insider.* February 22, 2017. Accessed August 23, 2017. http://www.businessinsider.com/former-ge-ceo-jack-welch-says-leaders-have-5-basic-traits-and-only-2-can-be-taught-2017-2

Bibliography

Atkins, Alexander. "Tag Archives: Origin of the Buck Stops Here." *Bookshelf* (blog). March 12, 2013. Accessed September 11, 2017. https://atkinsbookshelf.wordpress.com/tag/origin-of-the-buck-stops-here/

Baird, Kirk. "Pushing the Envelope: Oscar Winners Famous for Memorable Acceptance Speeches." *Las Vegas Sun*. February 23, 2004. Accessed August 23, 2017. https://lasvegassun.com/news/2004/feb/23/pushing-the-envelope-oscar-winners-famous-for-memo/

Blackaby, Henry T., and Richard Blackaby. *Spiritual Leadership*. Nashville, TN: Broadman and Holman Publishers, 2001.

Bridges, Kendall, and Starla Bridges. *Better Marriage: Against All Odds*. Carrollton, TX: Kendall Bridges Ministries, 2016.

Busch, Jack. "Hard Work in 5 Easy Steps: Understanding Perseverance in the Modern Age." *Primer Magazine*. 2012. Accessed August 21, 2017. http://www.primermagazine.com/2012/live/what-is-hard-work

Chand, Samuel R. *Leadership Pain*. Nashville, TN: Thomas Nelson Inc., 2015.

Chappell, Paul W. *Leaders Who Make a Difference*. Lancaster, CA: Striving Together Publications, 2009.

Clinton, Robert J. *The Making of a Leader*. Rev. ed. Colorado Springs, CO: NavPress, 2012.

Covey, Stephen M. R. *The Speed of Trust*. New York: Free Press, 2006.

DW. "7.12.1970: Willy Brandt Falls to His Knees." *Today in History*. Accessed September 11, 2017. http://www.today-in-history.de/index.php?what=thmanu&manu_id=1668&tag=7&monat=12&year=2015&dayisset=1&lang=en

"Eddie 'The Eagle' Edwards." Wikipedia. Last modified October 23, 2017. Accessed November 2, 2017. https://en.wikipedia.org/wiki/Eddie_%22The_Eagle%22_Edwards

France, Lisa Respers, Stephanie Elam, Jason Kravarik, and Dave Goldman. "Prince Had No Will, Says His Sister." CNN Money. April 26, 2016. Accessed August 23, 2017. http://money.cnn.com/2016/04/26/news/companies/prince-no-will/

Gladwell, Malcom. *Outliers: The Story of Success.* New York: Little, Brown and Company, 2008.

Hunter, Ron Jr., and Michael E. Waddell. *Toy Box Leadership.* Nashville, TN: Thomas Nelson, 2008.

"Jerry Rice." Wikipedia. Last modified August 19, 2017. Accessed August 21, 2017. https://en.wikipedia.org/wiki/Jerry_Rice

Kane, Libby. "Mrs. Fields Cookies: How Debbi Fields Built an Empire from Scratch." Accessed August 21, 2017. https://www.themuse.com/advice/mrs-fields-cookies-how-debbi-fields-built-an-empire-from-scratch

King, Martin Luther Jr. "I've Been to the Mountaintop." Speech, Memphis, TN, April 3, 1968. *A Call to Conscience: The Landmark Speeches of Dr. Martin Luther King Jr.* Accessed October 17, 2017. http://kingencyclopedia.stanford.edu/kingweb/publications/speeches/I've_been_to_the_mountaintop.pdf

Kouzes, James M., and Barry Z. Pozner. *The Leadership Challenge.* 4th ed. San Francisco: Jossey-Bass, 2007.

Levin, Paige. *Maryland Officer Buys Diapers for Mother Caught Stealing Them.* CNN. July 27, 2017. Accessed August 23, 2017. http://www.cnn.com/2017/07/27/us/cop-buys-diapers-trnd/index.html

Lewis, C.S. *The Chronicles of Narnia: The Lion, the Witch and the Wardrobe.* New York: Scholastic, 1995.

MacDonald, George. *The Marquis of Lossie*. Project Gutenberg eBook, 2004. Accessed October 26, 2017. http://www.gutenberg.org/files/7174/7174-h/7174-h.htm

The Man Who Stopped the Desert. Directed by Mark Dodd. 2009. Accessed August 22, 2017. http://www.1080films.co.uk/downloads/man-who-stopped-the-desert-info-pack.pdf

Maxwell, John C. *Good Leaders Ask Great Questions: Your Foundation for Successful Leadership*. Nashville, TN: Center Street Publishing, 2014.

———. *The 21 Indispensable Qualities of a Leader: Becoming the Person Others Will Want to Follow*. Nashville, TN: Thomas Nelson Publishers, 1999.

McChrystal, Stanley. *Team of Teams: New Rules of Engagement for a Complex World*. New York: Penguin Publishing, 2015.

McCullough, David. *The Path between the Seas: The Creation of the Panama Canal, 1870–1914*. New York: Simon & Schuster, 2004. Kindle edition.

McCullough, Donald W. *Waking from the American Dream: Growing through Your Disappointments*. Downers Grove, IL: InterVarsity Press, 1988.

Meacham, Jon. *Franklin and Winston: An Intimate Portrait of an Epic Friendship*. New York: Random House, 2003.

Phillips, Donald T. *Lincoln on Leadership: Executive Strategies for Tough Times*. Illinois: DPT/Companion Books, 1992.

Platt, Suzy, ed. *Respectfully Quoted: A Dictionary of Quotations*. Requested from the Congressional Research Service. Washington DC: Library of Congress, 1989; Bartleby.com, 2003. Accessed October 26, 2017. http://www.bartleby.com/73/465.html

Thomas, Robert J. *Crucibles of Leadership: How to Learn from Experience to Become a Great Leader.* Boston, MA: Harvard Business School Publishing, 2008.

Today I Found Out. "The Can Opener Wasn't Invented until 48 Years after the Invention of the Can." June 4, 2012. Accessed October 30, 2017. http://www.todayifoundout.com/index.php/2012/06/the-can-opener-wasnt-invented-until-48-years-after-the-invention-of-the-can/

Welch, Jack. "Former GE CEO Jack Welch Says Leaders Have 5 Basic Traits—And Only 2 Can Be Taught." *Business Insider.* February 22, 2017. Accessed August 23, 2017. http://www.businessinsider.com/former-ge-ceo-jack-welch-says-leaders-have-5-basic-traits-and-only-2-can-be-taught-2017-2